Bruce Collins, married with one grown-up son was London born, but now lives in a small village in the Lake District. A move prompted by increasing disillusionment with his job as a council officer, and with London life in general. Now retired, Bruce has suffered from OCD since childhood, and has made understanding this complex disorder a life-long quest.

WITH BEST WISHES

Bruce Collins

Dedicated to the memory of Dr M. Cutner, my Psychoanalyst from April 1982 to October 1987, who gave me the courage and technique to reveal and then understand that previously hidden from me.

Also dedicated to my wife who has to her best ability, endured life with a very neurotic individual for many years now.

Bruce Ian Collins

MY OWN EXPERT

AUSTIN MACAULEY PUBLISHERS™

LONDON • CAMBRIDGE • NEW YORK • SHARJAH

A CIP catalogue record for this title is available from the British Library.

ISBN 9781786293626 (Paperback)
ISBN 9781786293633 (Hardback)
ISBN 9781786293640 (E-Book)
www.austinmacauley.com

First Published (2017)
Austin Macauley Publishers Ltd.
25 Canada Square
Canary Wharf
London
E14 5LQ

Contents

Introduction

Put simply; this book is the story of my experience of suffering from the anxiety disorder OCD. But unlike many similar books this is not just a list of different symptoms, when and where they developed and the eventual relief of finding some form of professional help. Rather because of my natural belief that there was meaning behind my many varied symptoms; what follows is an in-depth study of the psychological motivation behind and reasons for, the development of my OCD and its persistence. Eventually I was to discover that in me the intrusive thoughts and impulses and the resulting compulsive actions (the very stuff of OCD) were due to an inner conflict between still active infantile parts of my mind and my adult self. In short, I learnt to become my own personal psychologist in order to both understand myself and survive mentally day-to-day, this undertaking and the personal insights it produced form the essence of this story.

Like a great many with this disorder I have spent a good deal of my life battling against various intrusive thoughts and carrying out unwarranted compulsive acts. Starting gradually in my childhood it grew until compulsive acts and rituals dominated my later childhood years, these were mainly associated with fear of punishment for being bad, self-punishments to ward off such a punishment, and fears of becoming ill linked to a fear of hospital. At the time of course I did not consider any of this as an illness; or indeed strange – it was just me, there were just certain things I had to do, combined with uncanny fears of punishment if I didn't. However, when I left school at the age of 15 the nature of the symptoms changed dramatically. After a period of general anxiety and later panic attacks, sudden intrusive thoughts began, the content of which were so completely contrary and repugnant to my rather timid and conforming personality, that it was no longer possible to deny there was something wrong with me. For unlike the earlier compulsions, which seemed to be all part of my known fears and existing belief system, these thoughts, which appeared to come out of nowhere, started to threaten the very integrity of my mind, with their anger, oppositional ideas and urge to violence.

Thus started my life long battle with myself, driven by my need to understand and the fear of what might happen next; I became an avid reader of psychology and especially psychopathology. Even so it took four long years despite my obviously strange symptoms, before I could accept I was suffering from an actual mental disorder. This hard won acknowledgement was then to cause me further anguish in the form of anxiety for the future and in the question; was I going mad? Fortunately, my symptoms expressed themselves so plainly that even though I lacked the insight at the time to understand them within a personal context, it was still relatively easy to see parallels between my disorder and what was described in the textbooks I studied. Thus in the summer of 1976 I finally admitted to myself that I must have OCD, or as it was then called Obsessive-Compulsive Neurosis. It never left me; the compulsions, the intrusive thoughts and the associated anxiety became part of my life, running in parallel with my normal everyday functioning. Eventually I sought therapy, I needed to make sense of this inner turmoil and understand why my mind in certain areas seemed to follow its own agenda. So in April of 1982 I began what was to become a total of five and a half years of psychoanalysis, Jungian analysis in my case, mixed with a good few aspects of Kleinian and Freudian ideas for good measure. Insight into my condition followed, illuminating the previously unknown inner processes and connections behind my symptoms. But these gains in self-knowledge were mainly intellectual, the associated emotions remained elusive and my symptoms continued to wax and wane, throughout treatment. Years after analysis had ended; four bad periods of heightened symptoms each brought not only more mental suffering, but also the profound insights that had hitherto eluded me. Within the turmoil of anxiety and extremely disturbing intrusive thoughts, I now touched the raw emotional power and experienced more directly than ever before… the infantile tendencies within me, which were to prove to be the disturbed source of the whole disorder.

The 30 plus years of introspection, experience and study of OCD and not forgetting perhaps the most important factor of 'being in here with it' have enabled me to develop an in-depth understanding of this disorder. From a personal perspective I now believe I know the events and circumstances in my early childhood, notably a very close relationship with an anxious, panicky and overprotective mother, plus a traumatic event that predisposed me to developing later OCD. I also now understand how leaving school precipitated the change in the nature of the symptoms, for this life changing event that represented another stage along the maturing process, threatened my dependence upon my mother. The infantile parts of my personality could or perhaps would not adapt to this change, I the young adult me having no direct knowledge of these parts first experienced their distress as anxiety feelings and then as sudden intrusions into my awareness; these unbidden thoughts representing the rage and fear felt by these still active infantile fragments of me.

For me I have come to visualize these infantile areas as forming a substrate of ideas and emotions beneath my adult conscious mind. This area remains beyond the adult inner eye of reason, in other words it is outside the conscious reflective processes and knowledge... it is therefore effectively unconscious. Nevertheless, this complex of ideas and feelings continues to influence and contaminate the adult personality above, by reacting to new events and relationships in ways that were laid down and appropriate in the past. In me the active unconscious complexes responsible for my symptoms appeared as two separate infantile areas, although later I was to discover that in fact they were opposite sides of the same child personality. Regarding them as separate here: one is a fearful, timid, mother fixed child, who was intensely fearful of hurting other peoples' feelings, and absolutely refuses to grow up, while the other is a child best defined by his anger, his perverse negativism and oppositional nature. Both of these aspects produced symptoms I experienced at a conscious level, for example both produced intrusive thoughts, although due to their different temperaments these were vastly different in character. From the angry child came sudden impulses to punch or kick out, while the timid, fearful child produced intrusive ideas about being lost and vulnerable, and doubts and fears about other people and the world in general. My adult self struggling to respond to all this 'stuff' thrust upon it, evolved all manner of self-imposed limitations and compulsive acts, designed to ensure that either I would not, or had not, acted on any of these ideas and impulses from within. But it would be wrong to imagine that this inner conflict was solely between these infantile parts and the adult me. It also raged on between these inner aspects themselves; for example, the timid, frightened complex felt threatened by and terrified of the angry child complex, as this anger (I was to learn later) endangered his relationship with mother. Hence when both were active the symptoms I experienced became very much worse.

It is probably obvious from my style of describing and attributing symptoms that I am not in agreement with some current theories that OCD is caused by an underlying biochemical imbalance within the brain. Personally I believe that for my OCD I am in a position to refute this idea totally, having discovered the psychological factors underpinning this disorder in me, which unaided by any other concept are more than able to explain my numerous symptoms. There may indeed be a number of causes underlying the characteristic symptoms of OCD, just as there are numerous ways OCD manifests itself, my early onset OCD (before puberty) for example, being different perhaps from those who develop it later in life. Fundamentally mental disorder may be described in two ways, firstly by way of a label based on the observable signs and reported symptoms, the medical/ psychiatric model; and secondly by way of the personal factors that have given rise to and influenced the symptoms in that individual to whom the label has been applied... this book concentrates on the latter. The psychogenic core of this disorder in me being dissociated autonomous aspects of my own mind following their own agendas, the dispositions of which were laid down in my early childhood. Consequently, I believe OCD is not just an isolated defect that can be plucked out or medicated away it is part of you, and perhaps an important part the essence of something useful, but as yet undeveloped and largely absent from consciousness. I for example was always a timid and over compliant individual (in this I sided very much with my timid child aspect) the self-assertion I needed to be more effective being locked away within my angry child complex. In certain circumstances where the adult me should have spoken up for myself, this complex seemed to act in my stead, but of course only in an infantile way, which I perceived at a conscious level as impulses to hit out. This book looks in detail at these dissociated fragments of past personality, traces their origins and describes their connection to later symptoms

Chapters one to four describe how my symptoms developed over time, giving examples of their changing natures and of the evolving external situations that would trigger them. These chapters are for the most part in chronological order, and are based on memories I've always known, others I recalled while in analysis (and via introspection since), and from family sources. Almost from the very beginning explanations and conclusions are offered to make the otherwise inexplicable OCD symptomatology understandable, when of course in reality I lacked for many years the ability to do this. Nevertheless, I have opted for this sequence of explanation rather than endlessly returning to each example again, once I had in the chronology of the book developed the necessary insights to legitimately do so. Many, in fact most of the symptom examples given although spanning many years and thus occurring in many different situations, have nonetheless very recognizable common themes. Despite this I have used several examples to prove each theme, perhaps too many; the poor reader may (initially I hope) think, but this is a deliberate action on my part, for by this means I aim to prove that there was a constant underlying structure that gave rise to the symptoms in response to the various triggering events I encountered in life. Although there are numerous illustrations these are but a small fraction of the total number of these 'constructions of my own mind' that have plagued and limited my life for well over 40 years now in all their various forms. Intrusive thoughts, unbidden images, sudden impulses and inappropriate emotions, are but some of the variants of unsolicited and unwanted ideas that have invaded my awareness in literally countless complex ways. Obviously the sheer amount of this pathological material accumulated over so many years cannot be all reproduced here or indeed in any book, without even the most initially interested reader dying of boredom. Thus I have for this reason selected the most readily comprehensible, while also choosing those with the best storylines to engage the reader more effectively as I attempt to justify via these examples my assumptions about this curious and infinitely complex disorder.

In chapter five I describe my initial experience of psychoanalysis and give other little insights into the relationship I had with Dr Cutner. Recorded symptoms and other related information from this chapter on... have specific dates as they have been either taken from my analysis notes or from my 'psychological diaries', which were started soon after I commenced therapy and continue to this day. The reader will quickly notice that many of the entries used in the book are not in their original chronological order; again this is for the sake of clarity, for I have selected those diary entries and those sequences of entries best able to describe and represent my varying symptoms, while at the same time provide insight into the disorder as a whole. Although my timid and mother fixed child aspect is mentioned frequently throughout the book, the dissociated source of my ego-dystonic symptoms, known eventually to me as Rebel, is the subject of a detailed study in chapter six. While chapter seven deals with the interpretation of a number of significant dreams over a period of some years. These are included because since dreams in general come from the totality of the mind that is from both conscious and unconscious areas, they are another possible source of self-knowledge. Certain dreams or more importantly a series of dreams may come to illuminate the same areas of inner conflict and dissociation, from which also emanate the symptoms of the OCD. The dream images and the inner story they tell then provide another avenue to approach and attempt to understand the nature of the complex functioning behind the disorder. During analysis and since, I have had many such dreams and once I had learnt to appreciate and interpret these they became an important tool in my search for self-understanding. Indeed, as should be apparent to anyone once they have read this chapter, my inner knowledge would be greatly diminished if it were not for the insights gained this way. The last chapter, chapter eight of which it could be said with some truth the rest of the book exists merely to justify, attempts to pull together the different threads running through the history of my disorder, each a facet of the personal manifestation of my OCD. Here using a largely psychodynamic framework I link my earliest experiences with later triggering events to show that despite appearing bizarre, bewildering and menacing; the varied symptoms of OCD can be understood, and moreover that this understanding may be of therapeutic use to the sufferer. It is within this chapter that I share my final overall conclusions of the cause and nature of my OCD symptomatology. Finally, to all those about to read beyond this introduction, be you fellow sufferers, worried relatives, interested practitioners or just curious passers-by, I hope you all find something of value from my story of a life marred by this very perplexing and tenacious disorder.

Chapter One

Childhood years... first symptoms

It's a summer's day in the early 1960s and in the garden of my family's home I am playing absent-mindedly when I inadvertently pulled some plants out of the ground, which to me meant I had killed them. Instantly an assertion appeared in my mind stating 'I would be dead in one year' which I immediately understood to be the punishment for my deed. Luckily even at the age of 7 I did not believe the prediction totally, it worried me, it frightened me, but I still retained the feeling that if I could just forget about it, nothing in fact would happen. This example is one of the earliest I remember clearly, it has the theme namely guilt and punishment that was to spoil and oppress my childhood years, and which would persist in one form or another well into adult life. Overall the symptoms of this period, were mainly compulsive actions in response to a few general interrelated obsessional themes, these seemed always to revolve around the following key issues and concerns:

a) A fear of becoming ill, linked to a terror of needing to go into hospital

b) A fear of having done or of doing something bad

c) A fear of being punished by God or some other supernatural being (because I had been bad or disrespectful); the punishment being most often illness of some form and thus going into hospital

d) Self-punishments invented by me, designed to ward off the above

e) The gain provided by being ill (if it was mild and not too frightening) by soliciting attention, sympathy and appearing different

f) The specific symptoms directed at my mother when my brother was born.

The following are a few examples in chronological order of how the themes listed above affected my life; they are all from before the age of Fifteen and a half, when leaving school evoked the abrupt change in the nature of my symptoms.

It's the summer of 1964 and an outbreak of typhoid in Aberdeen Scotland has put over 500 people in hospital, unfortunately that's where the family and I were going on holiday that year. I became very concerned about this, believing that just going to this place would result in me becoming ill, also as the infection originated from tinned corned beef I developed a fear of all tinned foods. By the age of 7 or 8 I had amassed a vast range of vague and naïve ideas about illness, fear of tropical disease for example prevented me touching a string of beads, which I knew had come from abroad. I was afraid of 'dirty air' from drains etc. and 'dirt' in general on my hands etc., due to ideas about germs. Mixed with this fear of becoming ill via natural causes was the fearful notion of illness as a punishment. The following event when I was about 9 illustrates this type. During a family visit to some cousins I stole a small toy car; in the course of the journey home I began to feel very guilty about the crime. I felt sure God or 'something' would punish me, and the nature of the punishment would be illness and the need for an operation. I wanted to take the car back but that was impossible, but I could not be allowed to keep it, so I threw it away as soon as I could in the hope this would evade punishment.

The above incident shows the typical me during this period in my life, all the essential elements of my later pathological thinking are present: guilty feelings, the belief I would be punished, illness/ operation being the form of punishment, and an attempt to self-punish to ward off this punishment by 'others'. Increasingly the punishment I faced for breaking the 'rules' became crystallised into 'needing an operation' this was by far my greatest fear... going into hospital and having an operation, and hence it became my ultimate punishment. The next illustration of an early compulsion clearly shows my fearful concept of God; my mother was in the habit of saying a prayer with me just as I got into bed and this had been the norm for some time. Around about the age of 9 I started needing to say the prayer again once Mother had left the room, now this should have been an easy task a minute more at most, but no, because I had to say it absolutely perfectly. That is, without any stopping, missing out words or any small mistake of any kind, because I feared that if there was an error something would happen to me. Thus, praying could take up to an hour and often did; going over and over the same little prayer until I was satisfied it had been said absolutely correctly.

A children's' encyclopaedia I owned was my next source of anxiety and ritual, for in it was a picture of an operating theatre with an ongoing operation. Seeing this picture despite my best efforts not to, would cause me to feel I too would have this fate and in order to prevent that, I felt the need to draw the illustration absolutely accurately any mistakes and I would have to start all over again until it was perfect. I can't remember how many times I drew that picture now but it took up a lot of my time and I hated doing it, nevertheless I felt I just had too. In the end just seeing this book (never mind opening it) would result in a compulsion to draw and for increased accuracy I ended up tracing the whole picture, a long and slow procedure. The book was eventually 'lost' that was the only way at the time I could remove the trigger that provoked the compulsive act. Within a year or two of this event the need for self-punishment was more or less always with me and would spontaneously appear. For instance, when I was playing with my 'Action Man' (a popular action figure of the time) it would suddenly occur to me that I would have to stop what I was doing for a certain amount of time, usually an hour or two during which I could neither go near or touch the toy. If I were not to obey this 'instruction' I felt something would happen, namely punishment by illness linked perhaps to the need to go into hospital.

On the 15th February 1967 my brother was born... I had just turned 10 years old. This event evoked a set of unique compulsions that were all directed at and associated with my mother. They started very soon after the birth, the first being my need to say sorry for anything however trivial that may have hurt or offended her feelings. Again if I didn't follow this through I had an uncanny feeling something bad would happen, thus I ended up saying sorry many times a day. I remember this episode very well and believe me I didn't want to keep on saying sorry, I was well aware that it was silly and I looked stupid doing it, nevertheless I felt compelled to continue. In fact, the compulsion was only laid to rest when my mother (obviously fed up with me) said suddenly one day 'it's no good keep saying sorry if you don't mean it' this input somehow broke the spell and after weeks of saying sorry, I could finally give it up. Closely related to this compulsion were two others, one was the need to confess or admit to any misdemeanour again however trivial, while the second was more of a passive affair, namely I felt I had to do everything my mother asked me to do… no buts no excuses, and if I didn't, the same feeling of punishment in some way would be evoked.

By the time I entered high school my earlier fears concerning catching a disease from dirty air, dirty objects or dirty hands, had resulted in a compulsive action to neutralize possible harm from these sources. So if without thinking I put my pen into my mouth, or dust was blown or dirty water splashed in my face; there at once followed a feeling that I would have to spit in order to get rid of any germs that may have entered my mouth. When possible this would be down a sink, drain etc., or into a handkerchief or paper… but the need became so frequent and in places where discreetly spitting wasn't really possible, that I started spitting down my jumper and some days after a lot of spiting there would be the obvious, uncomfortable consequences of a very wet shirt. The spitting compulsion later also became linked to fragments of glass if something had just been broken and objects like needles… in both of these triggers there was a fear that the items had somehow got into my mouth, thus the need to spit them out. I also hated small items 'disappearing' or more accurately not being able to account to what had happened to them, because of the fearful idea that would occur to me, that I had somehow swallowed them.

The above then even though drawn from only the more persistent and well formalized examples of my obsessional, compulsive thinking, clearly shows the underlying themes and how these interacted with one another. A particularly clear example being the symptoms in relation to my mother when my brother was born: it's plain to see that this relationship felt threatened when my brother appeared on the scene; after all I was being replaced… it was confirmation that I wasn't good enough. Thus I had to try to be extra good that's what the resulting compulsions attempted to coerce me to be. Their compulsive quality and my conscious incredulous attitude of them, indicating that they were not generated within my 10-year-old mind, but rather were the products of a much younger, more vulnerable vestige of me, still active within the older child.

Taking the age of 10 as a convenient point in my childhood I will now attempt to describe the nature of my personality independently of the overt obsessional aspects that besieged it, though of course in reality these obsessional/compulsive aspects were by this time firmly part of that personality. By any objective opinion it would be safe to say I was a timid, shy and anxious child, who lacked in both self-confidence and self-esteem; being mother fixed I was afraid to be away from my parents or home for any length of time, a fear that greatly affected my mixing with other children. Linked to this was a fear of growing up, which had been present in me from a very young age, I just never wanted to grow up and was nostalgic for anything left behind, even for example the previous year's classroom or the hall used when in the infants. A year later with the prospect of high school looming over me with all its associations with maturity, I voiced my concerns to my mother saying, 'but I don't want to grow up' which was met (and I've always remembered it word for word) with, 'Don't be silly you've got to grow up'... and there ended our philosophical debate.

Even though I always went, school remained a difficult place for me, for I lacked the ability to stand up for myself or be in any way assertive. I was afraid of the teachers and scared of the other children, whom I was afraid to cross or upset in any way in case they would turn against me. Thus I became a pleaser and a bit of a comic to survive and when these didn't work I hid in the library. But why didn't I have the ability to be angry, to stand up for myself... well in conjunction with the general circumstances of my childhood, there was a specific reason which resulted in me fearing my own anger and that reason was, my mother was afraid of any expression of anger and seemingly regarded it as a sign of madness, a view she openly made known on many occasions. Unfortunately, she found good examples of that fear in my father and grandfather, both of whom she regarded as having mad eyes when in a rage she even called those eyes 'the Collins look', something that left me feeling I too was condemned to have them. So it was clear to me from an early age that if I were to remain Mother's special good little boy, I must never have the same mad eyes of either father or grandfather, which meant of course I could never become angry. Within a few years my general fears of other people crystallized into a new form of symptom, one of a number that I was later to term my 'paranoid obsessions'. This first example of that category began when I was bullied at high school, I feared the main perpetrator might try to follow me home, and so began the compulsive need to suddenly turn round at frequent intervals on my way home, just to check no one was there. But it wasn't just other mortals I was afraid of, my fears concerning God and other supernatural beings continued to grow. I became concerned in general about always doing the right thing, what God would want me to do…obviously I didn't want to enrage him in case there were consequences. One conspicuous way this manifested itself was in my fear of religious pictures and other such items, when confronted with these I had an uneasiness feeling that I might in some way be disrespectable to them, thus I developed a bit of a phobia for these objects.

My general anxiousness and nerviness linked to my fears of illness resulted in me thinking every ache and pain I developed, was bound to be something serious. I latched on to all the TV dramas and documentaries about medicine, doctors etc. to learn more about illnesses and their symptoms; family stories of various ailments and different complaints, some of which ended in hospital treatments were also of great interest and distress to me. From these I learnt that my grandmother had, had appendicitis and a hernia during childhood and that my father had also had an operation as a young man, which for many years I believed was for appendicitis also, but in fact he too had suffered a hernia during his national service. Thus believing two members of my family had both been struck down with appendicitis I felt doomed to succumb to it also and of course suffer the subsequent feared hospital admission. If at any time I developed a stomach pain... for me it always meant the beginning of this dreaded condition, up would go my anxiety, inner questions such as, 'was the pain moving to the right' produced more anxiety. I would perform tests on myself like I had seen on the TV in order to prove my diagnosis and further panic would of course make the symptoms worse. This I understood, I was aware that if I could just relax and forget about it all I'd probably be alright, but the constant fear of hospital made this very difficult. The compulsive irrational nature of all this was well demonstrated by a very early compulsion which I still have a tendency to do even now; if a pain appeared to be situated in my right side I would have to touch both sides of my body six times. Why, what could be the meaning of this incomprehensible action, well there was a meaning to the child's mind that devised it, this action of touching both sides of my body was to disperse the pain equally across my stomach thus making it not a symptom of appendicitis. Fear of a hernia although always subordinate to that of appendicitis, nevertheless also made my life a misery, if I inadvertently lifted something heavy or pulled a muscle to my anxious mind a hernia could well have been the result. But it wasn't just the family's medical history that was a source of fear; the fates of other children could equally be as alarming. So when a boy in my class was rushed to hospital for what we later learned was a 'twisted gut', I became terrified this would happen to me and so developed a phobia of twisting myself round quickly or falling awkwardly least my gut would twist also. Another example was provoked by a visit to old family friends whose son had been ill with bad cough for some time; I listened in horror as they told my mother how he had recently been in hospital, because the inside of his chest had become 'beaten hollow' by the continuous coughing. Not only was I afraid to be near this boy in case I caught this terrible cough, but I now developed a fear of coughing in general and resolved never to cough too much ever again, lest I too ended up in hospital. My last illustration shows how even a book could be a trigger, the book in question being a biography of Marie Curie read to us at school. The latter part of the story details her death from cancer, identifying with this aspect produced a dread that I too had this terrifying disease and I developed 'burning pains' and other physical symptoms that matched my ideas of what cancer could do, curiously this scary thought would abate somewhat when I returned to the supposed safety of home.

But it would be wrong to conclude that my relationship with illness real or imagined was always negative... afraid as I was of the whole subject, I still enjoyed aspects of being ill, if and only if, I knew it was nothing serious or I had obtained enough insight to know it definitely was caused by my nervousness. When either of these requisites was satisfied, being ill got me attention, could make me look brave or just different from others and an aspect of my personality enjoyed these gains very much. Here are some examples how this need revealed itself in everyday life. Mostly because of my general anxiousness I regularly had abdominal pains, indigestion etc. for which I often had a supply of indigestion tablets. Now these I would take in a conspicuous way and if other children asked, I would be mysterious about them, implying they were important and that I was ill. Sometimes of course my various pains especially those I wasn't that sure of would result in me going to the doctor, here a quick examination would ensue followed by a bottle of tonic... that GP knew full well I was a nervous child. On leaving the surgery I would be relieved and happy for now I knew I didn't have a serious problem… but I still had an illness, after all I had been given a 'medicine'. One of the best examples of me 'enjoying' an illness occurred when my brother was born; by the time my mother had left hospital I had developed a rash, which necessitated another trip to the doctor. Here Mother and I were told that my spots were probably due to worry about her and the situation, for me this was a marvellous revelation for it showed how much I loved and cared for my mother, and the nature of it also made me different and special. It did indeed get me special attention as Mother tried to reassure and comfort me, saying how silly I was to have worried; thus I won special attention even though my rival had just been born. Unfortunately, this didn't last long, Mother soon learnt from the school that a number of kids had a rash; apparently it was just something going round, so my stigmata of caring and love just became a few spots as far as my mother was concerned… I was bitterly disappointed.

In summary I think most readers will appreciate how the underlying themes of my psychological distress were linked and developed one from another. The fundamental ideas and belief patterns that form these themes are of very long standing, in other words I always seem in essence to have had them. Thus I believe they formed and initially unfolded in the anxious, overprotective and largely exclusive relationship between Mother and me during the first four years of my life…they are therefore infantile in nature and expression. The fundamental or root fear here seems to be that of hospital on which all the others are built or linked. So considering this: associated with hospital is of course illness… in me this divides into two distinct fears, one concerned with becoming ill via contamination and germs etc., the other being the fear of becoming ill as a punishment, both of these generated their own related compulsions. But why did my general anxieties and fears manifest themselves in this particular way… well this book is all about understanding and I believe the reason is a certain event that occurred when I was just over 2 years old in 1959. In April that year I had a period in hospital for a circumcision, which for some reason was deemed necessary. Now this wasn't a long period, having been admitted on the 30th April I was discharged on the 2nd May, therefore my stay consisted of two nights only. Nevertheless, this event was a trauma, for this was long before parents could stay with their child in hospital, and I who was used to sleeping with the comfort of a dummy, even had this taken from me, as the nurses forbade its use and stopped my mother from leaving it. For any small child a hospital visit without the presence and support of Mother, where strange people, dressed in funny clothes, do strange and intimate things to you, would be without doubt a traumatic event. But I was already a vulnerable and fearful child concerned about Mother and myself in our anxious world together; to me (my child's mind at the time) this episode was one of abandonment, confirmation of my badness, and my punishment for that badness. This event took the mix of my doubts and fears of the time, and fixed them in a particular format that from then on influenced and coloured my childhood pathological thinking and symptoms. How do I know this...well it's one part of many that fits so well with the overall picture I have discovered of the nature of my OCD. But my conviction is not solely based on the abstract. During one of my periods of heightened symptoms in the course of which I don't mind admitting I was really very ill...I spontaneously recaptured a hugely emotional memory; a physically felt turmoil of absolute despair... filled at first with shouting for mummy, then crying and sobbing for her till finally this diminished into a wordless whimpering surrounded by a dreadful feeling of utter, utter despair and palpable fear. These episodes of heightened symptoms, which other sufferers of OCD will know only too well, always equate in me to my adult personality being close to the child 'substrate' underlying it, or what amounts to the same thing, this 'child' being particularly active so it is able to unduly influence and contaminate the adult. These episodes are therefore filled with renewed onslaughts of intrusive thoughts and emotion from the child, while the anxiety generated within the adult personality by these intrusions causes additional distress. But just sometimes they also offer the chance of further insight and understanding because one is closer to the source of the disturbance... much more of this of course later.

Chapter Two

Now I'm fifteen

As I entered my teens I remained remarkably childlike, fearful of the outside world, I still clung to home and my parents. In terms of obsessional/compulsive symptoms the themes established earlier persisted. I therefore remained afraid of illness via contamination and as a punishment, linked to the latter my fears continued about what God would want me to do, and consequently I continued to be over concerned about doing the right thing in everyday situations. Of course at school I had to act more grown-up than I could get away with at home, and as my chronological age increased this discrepancy between home and how I was outside, grew more marked. For example, I seemed a reasonable 13 or 14-year-old schoolboy, albeit one timid and anxious, when at school. But once returned home I markedly regressed, playing with my young brother, using his toys, and watching TV programmes such as playschool with him, and I must admit I enjoyed doing this. It was as if I needed and wanted to stay within the protected world of childhood. This change to a younger self was especially noticeable during school Holidays when I would rarely meet with my peers.

But change was on its way; it started when from about the age of 14 ½. I got in with a different group of boys at school. I seemed to fit in as I first identified with and then mimicked their behaviour. Now these were real lads in every sense of the term and being with them seemed to release a different me; more outgoing, jokey and carefree. In their company I quickly developed a new more mature personality, but unfortunately in a person as dependent and childish as I was this change was only superficial. In other words, this was pseudo-maturity with little foundation, precariously built upon my fearful, timid and mother fixed personality, unfortunately at the time I was not in possession of this important insight. Feeling grownup and wanting to be independent I began to dislike school even more, and for new reasons as my new persona resented the control and discipline of the place, I wanted to be free. So when one of my group told me he was thinking of leaving (you could leave school at 15 in those days) I immediately identified with what he said, although I had not previously considered it myself. The idea stuck in my mind and I talked about it at home, where there was a general indifference to the subject; both my parents had come from 'very ordinary backgrounds'; this was something they would freely admit, they consequently expected little from life and had aspirations to match, and these notions they easily projected on to the next generation. Drifting along and unhappy at school now with my new need for independence, plus the idea I could leave anytime I wanted, became a powerful cocktail of ideas and feelings; that was to lead me into quite suddenly leaving when a job in a local garage became available. This decision to leave school when I was just 15 ranks as one of the worst if not the worst decision I ever made, for never was there a person less prepared, less equipped for this important transition in life, but of course at the time I was oblivious to this.

I had a week off before starting at Greenhill Motors where I was to be working in the stores section with two others; it was a sort of holiday before the ordeal. By the end of this week I was feeling nervous to say the least. Never self-assured in new situations it was a very shy, timid and silent me that turned up for my first day at work at 8 o'clock that first Monday morning. All my fears and worse were soon realized, any pretence of being grownup and independent fell away within a few days. I just didn't know how to deal with my new workmates at an adult level; their general manner seemed to be aggressive and intimidating and I took everything personally. Of course I now well understand that what I was experiencing was just the normal banter and push and shove of the factory floor, but to the younger me the way I was spoken to and what I was expected to do was a real shock to me. With my grownup persona now in tatters all I really wanted was to be back at home; this made my 50-hour week, which included Saturday morning, seem like eternality... an eternality of shyness, awkwardness and increasing dislike of the boring routine. Whatever my childish views of working life had been, what I found myself doing now had no resemblance to the half thought out ideas and dreams I played with while at school. Then to make matters worse while at work I started having strange missed beats of my heart, which caused me to clutch at my chest as if my heart was about to stop. Obviously to the naive 15-year-old who had always been concerned about illness and hospitals these episodes of dropped beats were terrifying, and they seemed to get progressively worse with each passing day. Of course with the hindsight, I now know that the work environment was so stressful for me that it was causing symptoms of anxiety to develop; a typical feature of which are the effects on the cardiovascular system, namely tachycardia, palpitations and dropped beats. I did also have what I now recognise as other symptoms, for I was tense and agitated... but it was the physical nature of the missed beats that my personality was particularly sensitive to, and hence my fixation on that specific symptom.

When I had started at Greenhill Motors they had been informed and decided to honour a week's holiday that had been previously booked by my parents. So within six weeks of starting I had a week away, it was a godsend, although the first night I just couldn't relax my heart raced and continuous palpitations left me breathless and fearful. Laying there I was sure there must be something physically wrong with my heart, though strangely rather than telling someone and getting help I just remember thinking, well if I die now at least I'm with everyone. By the next morning the anxiety had left me and during the rest of the week I never suffered a single problem with my heart. I now understand that I was of course back in my comfort zone, effectively this week was like life before I left school, for once again I was back safe in the familiar, predictable relationships of home. But of course, as the reader will have probably have guessed within a few days on returning to work my anxiety and heart symptoms reappeared. Very quickly all the old negative feelings came back, plus I now began to feel very frustrated and aggrieved at the situation I was in, as for my parents they just didn't seem to notice my distress, after all to them a boring job was as good as any other... that's what ordinary people did. At home now my behaviour was also changing I became suddenly passionate about learning things; for me this mainly meant studying books on electricity, building working models associated with this, buying chemistry sets etc., and concerning myself with animal conservation. Now these efforts were no private affair all my studies became quite showy and ostentatious, for it was important that people saw what I was doing... most importantly that my parents saw what I was doing. So gained knowledge and diagrams of what I had achieved were placed on large sheets of paper, which became posters I used to decorate my room. What was the motive behind all this, well it may be obvious now but at the time I was just doing what felt right – I had no special insight nor did I even question the need, but years later while in analysis this tendency proved to be still active. Within the therapeutic relationship, the phenomenon of transference (basically treating the therapist in the same way as you did important people from your past) is an important natural development of the treatment process, and I had been quite unthinkingly drawing pictures and taking these and other things I had done along to sessions for about six months, before my analyst finally told me what she felt I was doing, and of course I was looking for praise and attention, just as I had done when I was 15. Unfortunately, at the time I was unclear of what I wanted, let alone being in a position to voice my needs. How much leaving school had stirred up deep and powerful feelings was yet to become plain to me and for my parents also, who remained (so it seemed to me) oblivious to my efforts to attract their attention; it was as if I was shouting albeit symbolically, "look at me...I'm here... look what I can do", but nobody heard.

My mood continued to deteriorate and at work now a feeling of angry frustration pervaded everything I did, this and the increasing episodes of palpitations made each day a misery. These feelings gradually spilled over into my home life, here too I felt agitated and frustrated and I would often walk round and round the lounge thinking to myself or even saying over and over again, I can't go on, I can't go on... my life is meaningless for me. In fact, one of my favourite saying of this period was a line from a then popular pop song, 'all my life's a circle' for me this summed it all up, this is what my life had become... an endless circle of boring work and home, and most of it was the boring work bit. I became very jealous of my brother after I was shown a photo of him and my parents taken during a family outing whilst I was at work, basically I wanted to be back at home like him, I felt forgotten disregarded, now I was grownup at work. Increasing desperate now to attract attention to my plight I began to act in a particular manner night after night. This behaviour seemed naturally to develop although there were aspects of it that were an obvious deliberate childlike ploy to get noticed. Thus most evenings after work I took on a non-speaking, non-responding stance in regard to my parents, which effectively meant, that for long periods I would just sit head in hands looking at the floor, as if in a deep depression. This then was how my last evenings whilst still at my first job were spent; gradually the mix of feelings evoked and accumulating since I left school began to overwhelm me: anger, frustration, bitterness and despair beset me, while the physical sign of my general anxiousness, my racing heart and palpitations become a constant accompaniment to my low mood. When feeling like this almost any additional stressor can produce a mortal blow to the already struggling personality, and my nemesis proved to be a forthcoming dental appointment. I knew I just wouldn't be able to face it... never at ease at the dentist at the best of times, with childish fears now crowding in on me I realized it would be impossible. So with the appointment looming large at the end of the following week, I made plans to disappear on Monday morning and not turn up to work. This I did by getting up very early and after carefully making my bed so it looked like it had not been slept in, I left the house before anyone else was about. My destination was London Zoo this is where I would while away my time to have as much effect as I could on my parents. Why the zoo? Well I had a genuine interest in animals and conservation; it was a place of interest and importance so different from my boring, irrelevant job. By the early afternoon I was making my way back as slowly as I could and soon after leaving the local station I was found by my father who was out looking for me and told to come back home. Once back the frantic questions began especially from my mother, where had I been, what was I doing, was I out all night... added to this was the continuous emotional accusation, we were all worried you know! My young adult personality already at breaking point now just dissolved; to me my parent's manner seemed hostile and uncaring they seemed more concerned with me having time off work than how I felt. When pushed to say what was wrong with me I just broke down into floods of tears and said that I just didn't feel safe. This emotionally changed statement 'I don't feel safe!' almost seemed to appear spontaneously from my distraught inner self and looking back now it did best represent the way I felt at the time, for truly I didn't feel safe in my new world of work and adulthood that suddenly leaving school had thrust me into. Many years later when new insights into this period had been won I was to realize that there was one aspect of my personality above all, which was particularly sensitive to this change, this milestone of growing up. This aspect at the time found expression in the floods of tears, in my need for my parent's attention, and most clearly in the feeling of not being safe. My time back home had begun; it was to last about three months until the situation there far from helping me, pushed me back out into working life, still unprepared and with most problems still unresolved.

After the initial questioning and probing of that first afternoon, things were left awkwardly unsettled, I couldn't explain adequately why I felt the way I did, for I didn't really understand what was happening to me. Subject to odd powerful emotions I just felt strangely small and vulnerable, scared of the world and needed to be home.

The next day my presence at home rather than being at work, brought back the questions, what was I going to do, what was wrong with me, again once under pressure I broke down in tears. My mother especially seemed over concerned with what other people would think, and kept on insisting that I should return to work and leave 'properly' if that's what I wanted. But it was all too late for anything like that as far as I was concerned, I just had no confidence anymore to face the world and the more pressure was applied the more unsafe I felt. As days turned into weeks my anxiety with all its associated symptoms remained high, it did not disappear as it had done when I on holiday, obviously the tense atmosphere at home was no longer conducive to me feeling supported and secure... the very things I was desperate for. Each day now my mother would have at least one period badgering me about being at home, questioning my intentions, urging me to get another job and reminding me I just couldn't stay at home forever. Eventually because I wasn't responding and also because I was complaining so much about my heart I was taken to the doctor, accompanied there by my mother and even my father, who must have found it all quite difficult for he was a more remote figure who didn't get involved in 'emotional' matters. The doctor was quickly told I had lost all confidence, refused to go to work and thought there was something wrong with my heart. To his credit he quickly dismissed my parents from the room and asked me what was wrong, unfortunately it was all downhill from then on for I lacked the insight to explain. So within a few superficial statements in just as many minutes it was agreed that I should change my job, take some tranquillizers and that was that... not the sudden breakthrough I think my parents were expecting. I returned home didn't even take the tranquillizers and the situation continued as before, but things quickly grew tenser now between my mother and me when it was obvious nothing had changed. Daily arguments erupted as the pressure on me to do something escalated; unable to understand the situation or me my mother continued to go on and on about me finding a job, how terrible it was to be out at work... to just sit about etc., and all the time I had this feeling she was more concerned with what she considered was correct, convention and what others might think, than my personal predicament. At this level of conflict, the atmosphere at home felt very hostile and strained this clearly had the effect of increasing my anxiety still further, until I was almost continually agitated and tense. In this state another symptom appeared. It was in the form of a dream like feeling that would suddenly come over me; when subject to this, things around me seemed unreal or strangely different. With hindsight I now understand this phenomenon as yet another psychological feature of anxiety, but at the time it was just another reason to start panicking about my overall condition... and ironically true panic was about to start. It was in December 1972 when my first panic attack occurred; without doubt it was one of the most terrifying experiences I've ever had, the first more so than the many subsequent episodes that peppered the years to come. That day the panic just seemed to grow out of my habitual anxious, agitated state, in a self- perpetuating spiral of fear I became more and more fearful for no discernible reason. Then it happened a peak of absolute terror broke over me, my heart raced, multiple palpitations shook my body and my legs turned to 'jelly', at the same time I felt overwhelmingly vulnerable as if I was about to die or go mad... intense feelings of dread and apprehension almost physical in strength displaced all other thoughts. In minutes the panic subsided but I was a changed person for it left a residue of fear, now I knew what being really afraid was like and worse still I didn't understand why it had occurred. Again only years later did I comprehend that the panic attack was just the pinnacle of the constant anxious state I was in, the cumulative effects of external difficulties and inner anguish had pushed me to the edge.

On the 31st December 1972 I turned 16 and a new year dawned, but January found me still at home, still anxious, crying and fearful. My mother's determination to do something was as strong as ever and her barrage of questions and ideas concerning what I should be doing continued, as did the resulting arguments. In despair she once again had me escorted to the doctor who was told bluntly, something had to be done, and so the following week found me attending a local clinic on the allotted psychiatric day. Here I saw a social worker once a week I can't remember the length of the session now, but we talked superficially about leaving school, what I wanted and life at home etc. If these sessions would have ever have been of help I was never to find out, for the problems at home and the pressure to return to work resulted in me only attending about 5 times. The atmosphere at home was by now intolerable as the relationship alternated between total conflict during the arguments and periods of silent toleration. Anger results as most of us know in hasty words and these disagreements were no exception, so a lot was said as my mother pronounced she just couldn't take any more of this! So accordingly my behaviour was said to be having a negative effect on my younger brother and it was mentioned that if I carried on as I were 'they' would eventually certify me. Thus the pressure upon me to do something escalated further and along with this a feeling of deep resentment of my mother's attitude developed, adding to the already existing feelings of rejection and abandonment. For me this new peak of conflict seemed to evoke an extreme unbidden angry reaction, as if from within a hatred of my mother revealed itself and easily found expression. Now when these arguments occurred they always ended with me screaming at my mother with real venom and enmity that I hated her…I hate you, I hate you, was said again and again. These were powerful feelings, rage stronger than anything I had ever experienced before, especially in regard to my mother. The result was always the same, more guilt as my mother responded by saying; I was hating the only person who really loved me. The situation already terrible went from bad to worse, daily feelings of acute anxiety interspersed with panic attacks and a constant general unknowing fear of what was happening to me, filled my waking hours. As for sleep, agitated and with heart pounding I found it almost impossible and when I did, it was fitful with early waking bringing me back to my fears. None of this though could I mention, for the tense state of affairs at home couldn't tolerate any more problems from me, my mother just desperately wanted it to all go away, while my father maintained his emotionally distance... I was alone with my symptoms.

There had been other jobs set before me during my three and a half months back at home; most my mother had procured, but now another become available located by a friend of a friend and the pressure to accept this one was just inescapable and so in the third week of 1973 I agreed to give it a go. I remember well my parting words to my social worker that final session, in reply to her question, how can you go back feeling the way you do, my utterly vanquished response was, what else can I do. Monday came and I went, it was small metal spinning company consisting of two men and a boy... and I was to be the boy. My main job was to cut circles of metal out of square sheets using a hand -operated machine; these were destined for the lathes of my older colleagues. I managed to hold it together while there and get through the day, in spite of feeling extremely vulnerable and fearful it almost was as if I was attending my first day at infant school. But once back home my adult facade dissolved and I broke down crying and shouting that I couldn't go back and what a terrible place it was. However, my mother's reaction was even more terrible and a dreadful argument ensued, during which she made it plain to my father and I that she just couldn't go back to how it had been, (me at home) and if he does come back, that bloody TV is going (our first colour TV had arrived a couple of months before) he's not going to lay there on that settee watching that all day long. On and on it went, the most bitter and distressing row so far, but in the end nothing was resolved. In disgust my mother left the decision whether I went or not to me and went to bed, followed by my father. I was left in a dreadful state of agitation, going to sleep was out of the question, with heart racing and plagued by multiple palpitations so bad I really thought I would be dead before morning, I walked about the house.

Despite my desperate feelings I dared not seek any help, I felt sure the family situation could endure no more from me. Eventually, I got to bed and did fall into a fitful anxious sleep. On waking, the decision I had to make was immediately with me again… was I going to work or not? But now strangely I felt different, something had changed within me… I knew I was on my own and I knew now what I had to do. Somehow the notion and hope of remaining at home, of returning to how it had been, had vanished. Along with this overnight disappearance a tougher persona had seemingly developed, gone were the crying and emotional appeals to my parents and so when asked by my mother, what was I going to do, my response was merely, I'm going.

So I was back at work, to my parents especially my mother this was the answer for if things looked normal, then they were. But for me moving on like this while not understanding what had occurred, while nothing had been resolved was to prove disastrous. Within a few months of returning, the compulsions of my childhood were to be joined by a completely different type of symptom, which grew out of this period of turmoil, these intrusive thoughts so angry and opposite to my timid conforming personality, were to me the first real indication something was very wrong. But all this was yet to develop when I returned to work that Tuesday in February 1973, it was a noisy place that little factory with the lathes going all the time and as my colleagues one of which was also the boss were much older than me, it was also a lonely place. Thus there was much time to think about my plight as I stood alone turning the handle of the metal cutting machine, as in childhood my thoughts turned to concerns about my health, of which now I had an additional worry, namely my mental health. After all, had I been to a clinic on the psychiatric day and had seen a social worker, worse still I was victim to strange feelings of fear and panic, there must be something wrong with me… was I mental? was I mad? This was now the question. This fear mixed with my simple childlike ideas about madness, resulted in me checking myself continuously for any signs of becoming derangement. For me these signs mainly included fear of hallucinations both visual and auditory, I became sure that if I had such a hallucination it would be absolute proof I was mad. This fear found expression in me via a compulsion to check, for example on hearing a noise of not obvious origin I just had to find the source of it to prove it was real and not just in my head. I had the same need over things fleetingly seen or perceived, I felt I just had to establish they were real external phenomenon or go on worrying that this was my first real hallucination. For related reasons I tried to suppress my daydreaming in case I sort of got 'stuck' in an imaginary world and thus lost contact with reality. Of course all this self-questioning about what was true or real and external to one, and what was internal and imagined, set me wondering about the nature of existence in general. Unknown to me at the time (due to my ignorance) my thinking and my tentative probing of the essence of experience was becoming more and more philosophical in nature. For if one is trying to be certain one is not hallucinating or deluded, it is at once apparent that an understanding of reality in relation to the human condition is required. Although I never gave up or lost the common sense view of what was real and what was not, to my horror and shock I found there was no absolute way of always knowing beyond all doubt, the nature of reality and one's perception of it. My pervious unexamined views held up to that time and the inner feeling that one just knew, no longer seemed to satisfy me, in other words my psychological doubts about myself had led to a caricature of philosophical doubt. At the time of course I had no idea such ruminations could be legitimate, as in the study of that branch of philosophy dealing with the theory of knowledge. For me during this period these uncomfortable notions only had one explanation, they were just another confirmation that something was very wrong with my mind.

Despite my numerous problems, the childlike displays of distress such as the crying and helplessness did not reappear, but one aspect from that period at home did stay with me, namely the anger that appeared in regard to my mother. So although I was miserable, timid and fearful I was also angry... very angry and this anger suddenly revealed itself in an episode at work, which (applying psychological hindsight) was to prove to be a very significant event in my life. The day in question started like any other in the workshop as usual I was in the smaller of the two rooms, just a doorway away from my two colleagues working on the lathes. Now turning a handle to get a round piece of metal from a larger square bit is boring and if you're doing it all day it's bloody boring I can tell you. Hence at this particular moment I was just standing by the machine looking at it in contempt and considering whether or not I should oil it, a procedure that offered at least some slight break from the monotonous turning of the handle. It was then on suddenly looking up that I spied my boss watching me from the door- way, he had a sneer on his face indicating that he felt sure he had caught me red-handed doing nothing, which of course he had. Nevertheless, there was something about that look that just infuriated me and I responded with an angry, 'yeah!' This one word said thus, more than hinted at its underlying meaning of 'well what are you looking at?' Something my boss didn't fail to recognize and he didn't take too kindly to it either. He responded by shouting, 'yeah, I'll give you bloody yeah' and then a terrible argument ensued, during which I was threatened with all sorts of things, the end sanction being that I would be out of the job at the end of the week. With that last remark he stormed out of the room to join the other chap, informing him in no uncertain terms, 'I'll give him bloody yeah!' and then proceeded to go over the whole incident again from his point of view.

Alone back with my machine and while turning the handle the emotional enormity of what had happened suddenly hit me, my mother's words and her voice saying them came back to haunt me. I had the Collins temper, the same mad eyes of Father and Grandfather... Mother would despair of me, I had lost my job because I couldn't control my temper, I had let her down, I felt utterly damned by this realization... what would become of me now. All this had occurred in the morning and by the end of the day my boss had evidently thought better of getting rid of me, so before I left that night he had a word, dismissed the whole affair as one of those things and had given my job back. Of course I was very grateful and eagerly agreed with all he said for the dreaded confrontation with my mother had been avoided, even so the event had left a personal legacy something had changed within me, something, which at first I didn't ever notice...later I realized my anger had disappeared. It was never to return in the same intense direct form in which it had first appeared during those heated arguments with my mother, or indeed as it reappeared in the disagreement with my boss. It had seemingly gone in a way similar to my childish crying and dependency that had left me when I was pushed back to work, now both of these aspects had vanished from my awareness. I now know that both were to return, but in forms that for many years caused me not recognize the significance of the feeling evoked during this period. The first to appear, effectively now as a symptom, was the anger; this was to reveal itself in the intrusive thoughts, which were so foreign and frightening to my timid and conforming personality. Later unreasonable fears about the world and paranoid type thoughts about people again in the form of intrusive ideas appeared, these were to be linked to the painfully afraid, super dependent childlike aspect of me, which had first openly emerged during that fateful period at home.

In summary I hope it's clear that the act of leaving school precipitated in me the period of anxiety described in this chapter. This event had the capacity to do this because my personality although adequate up to that point could not deal with this self-inflicted change to my life.

The anxiety symptoms and the flood of other emotions released were a consequence of this change and also an indication of my failure to adjust successfully to it. In other words, I suffered a breakdown in as much as I was unable to continue my normal life routine due to psychological reasons; in me this initially presented itself as an inability to deal further with the external world, linked to a childish wish to run home and be protected. Of course my parents didn't see a small fearful child when I returned home and refused to go back to work, only a rather strange and difficult fifteen-year-old. In their defence I didn't understand either at the time; the inner needs that drove me to act as I did, so I was hardly in a position to assist in their understanding.

Considering this episode in my life from a theoretical point of view it is in fact well known that changes in an individual's mode of life, especially significant, rite of passage type changes, can trigger periods of anxiety and confusion and such periods may themselves precede the development of other types of mental disorder (i.e. other than just anxiety symptoms) or lead to the exacerbation of an existing condition, which is what was to occur in my case. Much later on in my self-understanding I would come to appreciate that although these aspects of me, the fearful child and the anger, first overtly appeared at the age of 15 they were actually very long standing features of my overall personality, although ones largely absent and concealed from my young adult's awareness. Nor was this to be their only appearance, for on several occasions since these same aspects have reappeared in response to periods of stress and turmoil and with their appearance, spells of heightened symptoms have always followed.

Chapter Three

New symptoms... new fears

Within two to three months at this new job, despite my continued fears about mental illness and the associated compulsive checking, my general anxiety began to fall and the panic attacks became less frequent. Although still vulnerable and fearful of the world in general I began to feel more my old self again, unfortunately this brief respite was soon to be shattered by the appearance of a new type of intrusive thought that was strange and menacing, and completely different from my previous intrusive ideas that tended to evoke compulsions, which supported or even strengthened my existing belief system. The first example of this 'opposite' unbidden thinking was to occur quite spontaneously while I was riding my new moped (something my parents had got me as a reward for returning to work); out of the blue a sudden intrusive impulse to turn into the path of oncoming traffic occurred; it was accompanied by an image of this happening. Now of course this thought shocked and frightened me, for if it had resulted in an action I would have been surely killed; to the super safe, timid rider I normally was, it was a totally incomprehensible notion. But like most single events, after a few days of worry I was able to dismiss it as unimportant, a momentary aberration and no more. But the second example occurring a few weeks later was to trigger a reaction that was to last on and off for years.

While at work, once again mindlessly turning the handle of my machine, I fell into daydreaming (despite my fears of such imaginings) about still being at school. I imagined waking up one morning to realize that all that had happened to me, i.e. leaving school, the two jobs the problems at home etc. were all just a dream, and in fact I was still a schoolboy. I was thinking this over and somewhat enjoying the idea, when suddenly a questioning thought interrupted my reverie. It was in the form of an intrusive statement posing the question, how do you know you're not dreaming… its nature was something that in the years to come would become familiar to me, for this idea like other intrusive material possessed its own sense of conviction and importance. But this was the first example and I responded quite naturally answering myself with a, well I just know, yet within seconds of this response I realized it wasn't an adequate foolproof refute. I still knew I just knew and throughout I maintained this common sense view, but I also understood that this 'knowing' wasn't absolute proof; after all, one could dream one was awake and indeed when dreaming one didn't question whether or not it was a dream, you were just in it. Of course waking reality seemed more continuous and predictable than dreaming but nevertheless, from moment to moment, I couldn't seem to prove adequately to myself that I was or was not dreaming. At this realization my fears of mental illness and of going mad were immediately triggered, for surely a person who fretted continuously over something that most people just accepted, must be mad and so began months of frantic effort to find a solution to this conundrum, to answer my own strange spontaneous question.

When, despite my best efforts, no satisfactory answer could be found this single obsessive idea began by way of a nagging doubt to undermine my existing view of the world. Virtually always present, this doubt negated or spoiled my everyday thinking and robbed me of my motivation, for if one could not tell the difference between dreams and reality, then how could I know what was useful and worth investing in and what was not because it was mere fantasy that would vanish on waking. Thus the obsession persisted and although I always hung on to the common sense conviction that I just knew the difference, I was never able to convince myself I did beyond all doubt, which is what the obsession demanded... ironically I even dreamed about the problem. Of course these ruminations did not exist in isolation they readily mixed with my earlier confusion and fears of madness, and my need to prove what was real and thus not a hallucination. Only years later when in analysis did I come to appreciate and understand once again the philosophical legitimacy of my inner conflict, this time after I was directed to the work of the philosopher Rene Descartes and his quest for certainty, part of which mentions this problem of distinguishing wakefulness from sleep.

While still in the grip of my 'philosophical' obsession another intrusive thought followed some weeks later. But this was very different type of unbidden intrusion firstly because it was clearly triggered by and linked to an external event and secondly because of its life changing ramifications. For this single episode went on to be the prototype for a whole category of similar intrusive ideas and impulses that were to blight my life from that time onwards. For a day that was to be of such importance it started just like any other day at work; it was July and the weather matching the ideal of that month was bright and sunny. So as I often did at lunchtime when it was fine I went on my moped up to a local café/shop to buy a cold drink and some sweets. On taking the bike into the car park I passed a group of three teenage girls, by the time I had parked up and dismounted, these girls had come over to me and started talking much to my shock and consternation…be assured girls didn't normally speak to me. Anyway they were around me now saying things like, that's nice, that's very nice I must say etc. and thinking they must be talking of the bike I agreed with them. It was not until they had walked away laughing that on looking down I noticed what they were really talking and sniggering about, my trousers' zip was wide open. Left standing there I felt idiotic and sort of ashamed and these feelings were reinforced when on the return journey I found it necessary to pass these same girls. With head down as if trying not to be noticed I sped past them as fast as I could, as I did so I well remember feeling briefly angry. The next day with the experience on the bike still on my mind I decided to walk to the cafe and all was fine until on returning, I happened to glance up and to my horror noticed one of the three girls walking down the road towards me. I panicked I just didn't know what to do for I felt far too embarrassed to face her, I considered crossing the road but it was too late for that option as she was already far too near and thus bound to notice me and know I couldn't face her. Thus trapped I had no choice but to pass her, so I walked on with head down and eyes fixed on the pavement just wishing the ground would open up for me, when just at the moment I was directly opposite her a sudden thought flashed into my mind, of me punching this young woman as hard as I could in the stomach. Although undoubtedly sudden this was a complex thought of action, consisting not only of the impulse but also of an image of the deed, I even seemed to feel the consequence of the blow in my own stomach. This thought that seemed to appear out of nowhere stopped me in my tracks such was the surprise and horror of it; I immediately turned to check I hadn't actually hit the girl even though I was sure it had only been a thought. I stood there for some time watching her obliviously walking on, wondering what had just happened trying to understand, but it was beyond me at the time to find an explanation. Back at work and throughout the next few days the episode tormented me especially the guilt and I was continuously concerned in case I really had hit her, despite my rational arguments and my conviction that it had been only a strange thought. These worries eventually blended in with all my others and as it did not occur again in due course the experience slipped from my mind.

In fact, this wasn't to be the only time a violent intrusive thought would force its way into my awareness, four months later in November in very different circumstances the sudden impulse to punch returned once more. But before I relate this incident I want to share some insights gained much later while in analysis and after, concerning this first appearance. I have considered this event countless times in the years since so it is now difficult for me to comprehend how I was unable at the time, to connect the intrusive thought with the external event that triggered it. Let's be clear here this was not just a random thought for I had already met numerous people that day on the way to the café and in it, so although not formed within my awareness this thought was plainly evoked when I saw one of the individuals who had made fun of me the day before. I am sure that if I had not seen her or if the open zip incident had not taken place, there would have been no intrusive impulse. In other words, this intrusive idea could be understood in the context in which it appeared that day; it was one aspect of my reaction on seeing the girl, the other being in keeping with my timid, conforming personality the embarrassment and dread I readily felt. The only difference was the violent reaction was not consciously elicited I didn't even feel angry but yet I was, it was as if I had within me a separate anger that could react independently of the executive me and indeed there was one significant feature of this outburst that supported that belief, namely the way it was expressed. For I the young adult didn't feel the emotion of anger, there was no verbal outburst or any urge to remonstrate with the girl in any mature way, there was only the unbidden impulse to punch… a rather infantile way of showing rage and resentment, which indeed it was but more about that later.

As mentioned before the next appearance of this type of symptom occurred in November 1973 by this time I had left the job at the metal spinners and was on a government-training scheme at a local college with the aim of becoming an electrician. The initial training period was a block of seven weeks at the college before places at local electrical contractors were found for the practical, on site element of the training. The college part for me was just like returning to school, I enjoyed the school hours, which enabled me to watch children's' TV again and the general feelings of being a student once more. Hence when back home I was more content and at ease, but it was a different matter at college where my overt timid and withdrawn personality didn't mix well with my peers, I was apprehensive in their presence and over concerned with keeping in with them. I had of course brought with me my continuing anxiety, I even had a couple of panic attacks while in the class room a very difficult thing to endure, for not only are you experiencing the terrors of panic but at the same time one is desperately trying to maintain a semblance of normality in a very public setting. Even so I got by I enjoyed the subject and unlike the others who had all come straight from school I knew what rubbish jobs were available for the untrained and uneducated, so I became a model student, eager to use this second opportunity to learn all I could. When the first block at college ended I was found a temporary placement at a small local firm and after a week of driving round and helping the foreman I was told early on a Monday morning to attend a certain building site. Now I was quickly given instructions how to get there, the general attitude within the office being, get on with it, you'll be alright...but for me anxious and uncertain I still wasn't exactly sure of its location but I dared not ask again so away I went. A trip on the underground took me to the correct locality and then following the sketchy instructions I set off in search of the site, although quickly finding the correct road try as I might I couldn't find the actual site. The day's general apprehension rapidly turned to panic as I retraced my steps a number of times but all to no avail. At a loss of what to do my mind filled with negative thoughts, what if I never find it, what would they think of me etc., in panic I even phoned my parents but of course they couldn't help. In the end after one more try and walking a great deal further down the road that I had been instructed to use, I found the building site. That evening I returned home at about six o'clock, curiously my behaviour and mood had reverted back to how it had been during my first job, i.e. I said very little and just sat staring at the floor, seemingly my childlike show of displeasure and attention seeking had been rekindled by the difficult day.

The next morning, I had to return directly to the same site, feeling a little happier now since I at least knew the way I quickly reached the station where everything had gone wrong the day before. But today I was ok that is I was ok until I started down the road that led to the site, the road that yesterday had been at centre of my confusion and panic. Suddenly without any warning an intrusive thought in the form of an image flashed into my mind, urging me to punch a complete stranger in the stomach, who just happened to be passing me at the time. In its mode of appearance and content this thought was almost exactly the same as the one directed at the young woman four months earlier and its effect was similar too, once again shocked and horrified I checked to make sure nothing had really happened despite knowing quite well it hadn't. Walking on again I was immediately in for another shock, for the intrusive impulse proved not to be an isolated event but reoccurred each time I had to pass someone, strangely though on reaching the site the symptom just disappeared. On returning home it reappeared but again only in that particular road, when on the next day it all happened again my fears concerning myself grew, I began to expect the symptom and fear it appearing, the simple walk to and from work became almost unbearable. I began to view myself as potentially dangerous, what if I really did hit out, to limit this or at least make it more unlikely I put as much space as I could between myself and passing others, to the same end I either held my hands together or thrust them deep into my pockets anything to slow down any possible action in response to the intrusive thoughts. Guilt now began to mix with the fear thus I felt compelled to check the well- being of each and every person a thought had been directed at, if for some reason I couldn't do this the fear and guilt that they might have been actually hurt persisted for days, although at the same time I retained the knowledge that nothing had really occurred.

So why had this intrusive impulse to punch returned now in this new situation and why was it different (i.e. it wasn't a single event) from the time when it was directed at the young woman. Well once again drawing on insights gained much later I believe it is possible to comprehend how this thought although apparently spontaneous and certainly unbidden was linked to the situation and place it began and in this case continued to occur. The explanation requires consideration of two elements, what had happened the day before and the return to that same location the following day; remember I had already walked past hundreds of people with no problem, it was only when I turned into the road where the day before I had become lost and panicky did the symptom appear, and just like when I reached the building site, the symptom disappeared when I was no longer in that road. Each day for about two weeks (the total length of time I was at the site) the intrusive thoughts began when I walked that road going to work and returned on it from work, proving this stretch of road had become emotionally significant to me due the distress on that first day. So unlike the first incident when seeing the person who had offended me triggered the impulse, in this second example it was returning to the same place that was the trigger. But why would that situation provoke an impulse to punch complete strangers, well I believe that can be understood if one examines the state of mind I was in once I became lost. Very quickly the stress of that day caused the young adult me to founder, overwhelmed with feelings of despair and helplessness, and ashamed of my own inadequacy I rapidly regressed into a childlike state, similar in nature to the one that had me running home from my first job; the verification of this being how I behaved that evening on returning home. On returning to the scene I was subject to yet another childlike reaction but one this time totally opposite to the timid, passive state of the previous day; for the intrusive impulses to hit out show an anger obviously related to the same event, finding expression in an infantile way. As long as I remained in that road I was effectively immersed in the trigger event and the anger thus evoked continued to source the intrusive thoughts, of course at the time I comprehended none of this, all I knew was these bizarre thoughts frightened me and threatened my integrity. On looking back now it is clear that a change to my symptoms had by this time already taken place, the compulsions that dominated my symptomatology prior to my breakdown had been extensions of my known personality traits, i.e. they either reinforced my various fears or maintained my conforming, passive nature, but their content never threaten my sense of self.

This all changed after my breakdown and the period at home, the symptoms now were antagonistic and at odds with my personal thoughts and values; as for example in the impulse to turn my bike into oncoming traffic this was obviously in opposition to my normal thinking. Also the first intrusive thought to punch the girl was completely opposite to the embarrassment and awkwardness that preoccupied my conscious mind at the time and the example above where feelings of vulnerability and confusion were replaced with angry impulses the following day.

By January 1974 the first work experience period was over and I returned to college for another study block, once away from the triggering location the intrusive impulse to punch had disappeared and since then I had, had a respite of just over a month without any particular symptom. But it had left a residual fear that added readily to my other fears of being mad, for how else could I explain having thoughts I hated having and which caused so much anxiety and guilt... there had to be something wrong with me. Once back at college I didn't have to wait long for that to be confirmed, for within a couple of weeks the intrusive thoughts were back and being directed this time at people I was with all day long. Again, I will relate this account with the benefit of psychological hindsight to help the reader to understand the significance of the symptom in the context of its appearance.

On returning to college I had tried to continue a friendship I had initiated during the first period, unfortunately it hadn't been much of a friendship even then, for it was obvious I didn't measure up to what this other lad expected, but there again the immature me didn't really measure up to adequately 'knock around' with any of my class mates. Nevertheless, I desperately needed to be friends with someone, so I hung on to him despite his increasing negativity towards me, which increased when he linked up with another student further distancing me. From now on I was on the edge of these two, often three of us together, but really only two in the group... they tolerated me just and showed it.

Looking back now I can completely understand this rejection for I was passive and clingy, no fun whatsoever to be around, and in order to keep in with others I had reverted back to my school survival technique of being a pleaser. Of course being with my so-called friends was no fun for me either, knowing they rather I wasn't there and being the butt of jokes and ridicule I nevertheless still put up with it because it was better than being alone.

Then one day quite suddenly, while I was standing with them in the refectory feeling isolated and awkward, the intrusive thoughts spontaneously appeared again. They were first directed at my friend but then quickly spread to his new mate, again they were almost identical to the other two episodes; sudden impulses with associated images, urging me to punch my companions in the stomach. Once again they persisted and every time I was with the other two the thoughts returned and stayed, which meant that in parallel to my normal thinking and interaction I was assailed with continuous thoughts of punching them over and over again. It is rather ironic really that an individual as timid and passive as myself and one totally lacking in any normal self-assertion, should at the same time be subject to such unbidden thoughts of violence.

Within days a kicking impulse added itself to the punching one, so now I had to worry about my feet as well as my hands, and as before I started using various protective measures against the possibility of actually carrying out a thought. Hence I would continuously monitor myself carefully, keep my hands in my pockets or at least hold them away and more awkwardly stand apart from the others, all done of course while trying to maintain a normal look and conversation. These consciously considered reactions to the spontaneous thoughts, although understandable as a natural response to the threat to me from within, nevertheless paradoxically seemed to strengthen and spread the original symptom. If for example I was anxious that in a particular situation an impulse to punch and kick might occur, occur it did, and the very act of monitoring and restraining myself seemed to provoke the unbidden thinking or at the very least maintain my concentration upon it.

I am now aware that this appearance of symptoms at the college was in fact to be the last time, intrusive ideas were to occur without a conscious system of protective measures waiting to receive them, and as this system grew in complexity over time so did the unwanted thoughts that gave rise to it. As for these particular thoughts they were destined to go on for the years I remained in contact with the other two, true they would wax and wane, but a sudden thought of violence was no stranger to me as I passively accompanied my friends on a night out.

In summary this chapter describes the origins of a new type of symptom that appeared after my breakdown and period at home; essentially these symptoms in the form of intrusive thoughts were oppositional and challenging to my conscious personality. Due to their oddness and their urging to violence they seemed to threaten me from within and hence caused further anxiety and confusion. When describing the situations in which the different violent impulses first occurred, I hope I've been accomplished enough to demonstrate to the reader, (in line with my own belief) that the intrusive thoughts had meaning in the context they appeared; i.e. they were not just randomly triggered by some neurological disorder. Rather I see them as the product of mental processes that took place beyond my awareness, true the resulting intrusive ideas were in conflict with my consciously held attitude and were expressed in an infantile way, but nevertheless were on reflection comprehensible and relevant to me as an individual and the situation they appeared in. Due to their nature I began to regard myself as potentially dangerous, fearing that the thoughts would lead to corresponding action, this concern I feel is a natural and totally understandable response of an individual's mind, subject to such material thrust upon it. Understandably then counter measures designed to negate and check upon the intrusive thoughts and the fears associated with them, are consciously evolved, these protective measures started in my case as simple increased self- vigilance and restraint; but were to go on to develop into a compulsive and restrictive system every bit as limiting upon my life as the intrusive ideas themselves.

Chapter Four

Symptoms evolve and proliferate

By the end of 1974 I had left the college course and was now employed full time with the same small electrical contractor I had done the onsite training with, here I was now an apprentice electrician with most of my training on site while continuing to go to college once a week. Obviously the different sites on which I worked, a mixture of domestic and commercial premises, could be close to home or distant; the people I worked alongside were boisterous and straight talkers, some were tough and aggressive and this included many of my electrical colleagues. You had to be one of the boys to fit in on a building site, not a <u>boy</u> like me. At the age of 17 I was still just as timid and anxious in a new situation, especially one a long way from home as I had been when left school, and as for dealing with my rowdy hard drinking work mates on equal terms, I might as well had asked for the moon. This being different from the others was not helped by the continuing angry, violent intrusive thoughts that made regular appearances in stark contrast to my timid and passive everyday persona.

These years just after the initial appearances of the sudden impulses were a period where this type of symptom grew rapidly, within months almost not a day would pass without some type of intrusive thought, most of them were the now traditional unexpected thoughts to punch or kick at those around me. But these were soon to change both in nature and strength, as before at college my conscious concerns and general anxiety over what might result if I didn't watch myself carefully, seemed to be an influencing factor. One of the first changes to occur was that the thoughts started involving the use of weapons and the first 'chosen' was the hammer, something of course I had in my toolbox, as did nearly everybody else on site. So now some of the intrusive thoughts consisted of images of me hitting out using a hammer, thus more anxiety... well panic really as I considered the real possibility of being mad or at least of going mad. In consequence I developed (quite understandably) a fear of hammers, which often made doing my job very difficult, soon just using a hammer or even seeing one would immediately trigger thoughts to use it in anger. Once again I feel the need to inform the reader of my utter abhorrence of these thoughts, although I acknowledge it isn't probably necessary to state again... nevertheless these strange uninvited thoughts seemed to threaten my very identity, both morally and of what I had come to naturally assumed was the essence of me. They made me feel unsafe with myself, fear myself profoundly and the resulting extreme anxiety, demonstrated just how much one can fear a threat from within and after all you never escape from yourself. Unfortunately hammers were just the start of this type of escalation, with me consciously acknowledging I couldn't trust myself, anything pointed, heavy or sharp became a potential weapon and if I feared it would be, then very quickly an intrusive thought using it as such would appear. But it wasn't just different objects that represented possible danger; certain locations could do that as well, being high up or by a river or a railway might provide an opportunity for my dangerous impulses to find expression, and indeed in such locations I had intrusive thoughts about pushing people off, into the water or on to the tracks; I even had the same images and urges directed at myself, for once again if I feared it, it would appear and persist as an intrusive idea. This proved to be one of the fundamental truths of my OCD, the internal generator of my unbidden thinking always produced thoughts that were the very opposite to my consciously acknowledged feelings and held views, and although this is obvious to me now it took years to see the connection clearly. There is something uncanny about a thought the production of which one has not had any active involvement with, for the resultant thought, image or impulse, seems to possess a certain extraordinariness; a self-importance linked to an emotional insistence that it is true or its needs imperative. All this remains so, despite the individual's awareness of the craziness and destructiveness of the intrusion and their best efforts at rejecting it. This is one reason why I believe such thoughts are difficult to understand in an ordinary, common sense way, their omnipotence demands a response on their own terms a response, which of course may be just as pathological.

The content of the intrusive thoughts was not the only aspect to evolve; the aftermath need to check also continued to develop, becoming more complex and bizarre. I have already mentioned in the last chapter how I felt compelled to check on the individuals who had fallen victim to my impulse to punch, in order to confirm I had not inadvertently carried out the mental image. Looking back to check once, soon felt inadequate so I began to do it twice and then three times... this need to check was compulsive I just had to do it, despite being critical of it and knowing it wasn't necessary. Very soon I was checking on anyone a thought had been directed at a number of times, if someone disappeared from view (especially if didn't see when they went) before I could complete my checking I would feel particularly guilty; for it left me feeling I had indeed carried out a thought and this 'conviction' would hang over me for a few days, during which I also would have a nagging fear of some kind of resulting punishment. This check ritual became even more bizarre when for example I felt I had knocked people over with a particularly hard hit or push, in response to these impulses I often felt compelled to check the pavement or floor to make sure the person concerned wasn't lying there. Again I often had to scan the floor a number of times even though a quick glance would have sufficed to be fully sure no victim was really there.

Eventually, another complication became associated with this careful scanning, when in response to an intrusive idea I developed a fear that I might see someone lying there even though they weren't. This notion of course added yet another complication to the checking ritual; for now I was also concerned whether or not I was hallucinating and if I was, then surely it was even more likely in my 'madness' that the intrusive ideas would eventually breakout as actions.

The rest of this chapter recounts in detail some of the symptoms that marred my life during this period. The details are drawn from my psychological diaries (which contain information of symptoms, triggers and other related notes over a period of 30 years) or from the substantial notes I made during analysis, and although the violent type thoughts were the most troublesome they were not the only type, and it is with these more varied symptoms I will start.

My timid and anxious personality was never happy to be far away from home and if a site happened to be a considerable distance away then I became very apprehension to say the least. One such job occurred in the summer of 1975 when the company was working on new mobile classrooms at a school in Hornchurch, luckily I had recently started driving but the journey was to take me right across London. The first time I went was direct from the office, I of course got lost, became panicky and hated every minute of the nearly two-hour traffic congested drive.

The next day I left straight from home expecting the worst and got it, and despite being in my own car and doing ok really I nevertheless felt vulnerable and fearful trapped in the traffic in areas I didn't know. Then as I sat there wishing I wasn't the intrusive thoughts started, this time the mental images were of me jumping out of the car, leaving the door open and just running off, along with this came an impulse urging me to do just that. Of course this was everything I wouldn't do and so I began to panic as thought after thought tormented me, every time I had to stop due to traffic a new batch would start up. Fighting the thoughts all the way, knowing if I yielded to them they would make me look stupid and draw unwanted attention, I made my way to the site, once there the symptoms associated as they were with the journey only, left me and the rest of the day I was fine. But the next day they were back and back they were for every trip to this particular site especially if it was a slow and difficult drive, the only thing that did mitigate them somewhat was my increasing confidence with doing the journey. A month later a different symptom appeared this time during a holiday with my parents and brother. My father had always been interested in railways and industrial history and to some extent so was I and so on the last Friday of the holiday we walked the track of a nearby long disused mineral railway. Part of this was via a steep incline where the trucks would have once been pulled up on cables by a stationary steam engine, this was a very overgrown and lonely place and it had a strange feel about it of which even my father remarked. On returning I thought no more about it until in bed that night, it passed through my mind how frightening it would be on that incline at night, at once an intrusive thought flashed into my consciousness, stating that I would go to that location straight away. Once started, it came again and again urging me to jump out of bed and walk all that distance in the dark back to the incline, it was an absolutely ridiculous and crazy idea but the urging was real and terrifying, because the place I wanted least to go to at that moment was that uncanny incline. These two examples show that my intrusive thoughts were not always directly violent in content; even so they still caused me distress because of their oppositional nature. Although in the first occurrence of driving to the site, it isn't quite as clear-cut as me versus the thoughts, because I too hated driving all that way and didn't want to be away from home. Nevertheless, of course I felt constrained to carry on whatever I felt and my timid, conforming personality easily fitted in with that. The intrusive thoughts in this case seem to represent a similar if more extreme version of my dislike, how else could one explain the impulse to abandon the car and run away, other than as an intense anger and frustration at the situation and wish to escape it. The other example is much more polarized; I was fearful of the incline as I willingly fantasized about being there at night, while the intrusive thoughts seemingly triggered by this fantasy urged me to return. They were therefore totally opposite to what I would have wished to do; these symptoms also contained an element of self-frightening, something I would notice time and again in other similar unbidden ideas.

The next example, which was linked to one of my two 'friends' I had met at college, resulted in a truly pointless and bizarre checking compulsion that was to last for months. A bit of background is required to explain the triggering event adequately, by this time one of the two fellow students I had met at college had moved away, unfortunately he was the one whom I felt I got on best of all with. The other lad now had a steady girlfriend but because he didn't have a car he still deigned to go out with me every Saturday bringing his girlfriend of course, this went on for some time I would pick them up and take them back home and play the gooseberry in between. Gradually I began to resent this and feel used; it was at the end of one of these Saturday outings that this particular symptom appeared, I had just dropped of my two passengers, when just before I drove off a thought occurred to me, stating, I'm glad to see the back of them, such was the conviction of this that I half said it to myself at the same time. Moments later an insistent and tormenting idea suddenly appeared in my mind, urging me to check the car to make sure my friend and his girlfriend were no longer there, despite me certainly knowing already they weren't. This thought, although it lacked the anxiety provoking effect of the violent impulses, still possessed that strangeness and compulsive insistence of its own importance, typical of an intrusive idea.

All the way home I fought with this ridiculous thought and as usual rational conviction was no defence, thus I felt compelled to look time and time again as carefully as I could around the car. Once triggered this compulsion in common many others became displaced from the original situation to blight others, and indeed very soon after returning home a situation developed where I felt the need to check that my parents were not in the same room, even though I knew perfectly well they weren't. Can such a senseless idea and its absurd compulsion have an understandable meaning… well yes it can although at the time I was as baffled as is probably the reader. Years later it was examples of this type of symptom formation that led to the appreciate that my internal generator of unbidden thinking, was not only capable of angry and oppositional thoughts, but could in certain circumstances produce ideas and impulses that were just more extreme versions of my nature and consciously held views. What happened in the car that night was of course triggered by my expression of relief, spoken almost out loud, an aspect of me even more submissive and afraid of others, than the adult who had uttered the words reacted to this and was fearful they may have heard, this then was the origin of the intrusive idea to check. Clearly in response to the demands of my inner fears I was checking that my passengers could not have possibly heard my words. These compulsive ideas are emotional formed and maintained they seem to represent the fear underlying them rather than being a legitimate attempt to alleviate the feelings, thus no amount of checking ever appeases them... they remain beyond reassurance, also in me these aspects were infantile in nature and young children don't think like adults, but more on this later. So my duality within produced polarized symptoms, the angry oppositional thinking on the one hand and the fearful timid aspect on the other, both produced symptoms when triggered, the former mostly by way of intrusive thoughts while the latter mainly found expression via compulsive demands. In the next example, which is another instance of sudden violent impulses, both aspects of my personality the passive and the angry are plainly apparent.

This upsurge in symptoms, which occurred in the summer of 1976 proved to be, due to their nature and effect the most violent and disruptive of any prior to that date. For not only did they consist of the usual sudden intrusive images, this time an actual feeling of anger appeared as well, in others words I felt angry even though I didn't know why and this made the impulses associated with the intrusive thoughts additionally difficult to deal with. I was in a rage with thoughts of violence urging me to action; surely this meant I was a dangerous man… at risk of going mad at any moment. Such was my reaction to the impulses and the terror they induced in me as I fought with myself in order to resist them, that they triggered panic attacks.

As before I will set the scene by describing the series of events that led to the precipitating situation enabling the reader to hopefully understand, as I was to do years later how and why these particular symptoms appeared when they did. Still with the same electrical contractor I had joined after college I was by now a more senior apprentice, I had for some reason become split off from the electrician I normally worked with, and consequently had been sent to join some of my other colleagues at a site they had already been at for some time.

On arrival I discovered the job was at an old nineteenth-century school which was in the process of being converted into offices. In fact, the buildings, their internal layout and some of the remaining furniture greatly reminded me of my old primary school at Harrow, which especially initially, had not been a very happy place for the super timid and anxious me.

It was while standing there daydreaming and reminiscing of this, that a younger apprentice from my firm came over to inform me, in no uncertain terms that it was customary at that site for the last apprentice to join, to have the duty of going down to the bakery each morning for everyone's roll and sandwich requirements for that day. He then added it had been his job, but now it was my turn! I at once felt very indignant, thinking to myself how dare this much younger apprentice tell me what to do, feeling thus I responded by saying, I don't care who's doing it... I'm not! But this only made him argue all the more and becoming more and more angry he protested that he had, had to do it and so should I. At this point I broke away from the disagreement, the issue still unresolved; personally I had been shocked and a bit intimidated by the boy's sudden anger, and I was now feeling scared of the consequences and what the other apprentice might think of me – I began to wish I hadn't refused so blatantly. Indeed, later that morning just before tea break, despite all I had said and feeling pushed into it, I did indeed go down to the shops returning with bags full of rolls and sandwiches for everyone.

The next morning, I was again expected to carry out the chore, which I did, returning to site shortly before tea break weighed down with bakery products again. It was just after this break when I had returned to my work area that a sudden strange feeling came over me; it was as if I was terribly upset or angry about something, but I didn't know what... for I only experienced the emotion, there was no linking or explaining thoughts present. Within a few minutes of this the intrusive thoughts began, and in their usual form of sudden images they seemed to urge me to extreme violence, by showing me hitting out at the men around me with the hammer I was using. So strong were these impulses and the accompanying feelings of hatred that the fear I might actually carry out the idea, first led to extreme anxiety and then quickly on to outright panic. Thought after thought forced itself upon me; shaking in terror and believing that at any moment I might lose control I endured the mental storm, hiding not only these feelings from all around me, but the terrible anxiety they triggered as well. The whole episode lasted about an hour before disappearing almost as quickly as it had begun, but the residual anxiety hung on for the rest of the day.

The follow morning straight after tea break the thoughts returned, just as violent and extreme as the previous day. Although now the unbidden images that flashed into my consciousness contained the additional element of me running amok throughout the whole site with my hammer, these intrusions went on for some two to three hours leaving me in a state of total confused exhaustion. They even changed in content during this period, for by the end I was besieged by a sinister idea of going all the way back to the company's headquarters to attack my boss. Fearing this, I at least had the reassurance of knowing he was a safe distance away, but on considering this obstacle, an intrusive thought/image immediately appeared showing me jumping into my car and driving off to do the deed, yet another possibility to be resisted and be terrified of. The next day the same thing happened again and at the same time, for some reason, which I am completely unable to fathom now the intrusive thoughts always managed to catch me off guard, even when a cursory observation of them would have given me a likely time of their appearance. The only way I can possibly explain this is by acknowledging that at the time I always shied away from my symptoms and when present I was just at the mercy of them, and if they didn't occur I was just grateful to be free of them. It was only during analysis did I deliberately and very warily turn my attention to them, and begin to see them in the context of me as an individual, and the situations in which they were likely to appear. These violent 'tea break' symptoms were to appear about four times in total, before moving on to a new site brought welcome relief by removing me from the trigger situation and location.

So what explains this set of symptoms so violent and unforgiving that they reduced me to outright panic, well just before this episode I had in fact been fairly free from troublesome symptoms for some time, although the usual, in the background level of intrusive thinking and associated compulsions had continued unabated, but without causing too much anxiety. Therefore, there was something about that site and what happened there that changed all that. Firstly, there was the school buildings; these greatly reminded me of my own school and how I had felt there. Secondly and much more importantly, there was the heated exchange between myself and the younger apprentice, this more than anything else I believe, was the trigger event for all that subsequently took place. Unusually during this confrontation I had at least initially stood up for myself, feeling indignant enough to show some anger at the younger man's demands. But, no doubt helped by my adversary's anger this stance didn't last very long, within seconds of breaking off the exchange I was beset with guilt and fear over what I had said and was especially concerned of what he now thought of me. These doubts consistence with my usual timid and passive personality quickly led me to acquiesce and do what had been told, despite my quite conscious resentment and opposition.

The next day these feelings conflict had vanished and I was quite resolved to my task of shopping for everyone, although I did acknowledge to myself that my complete capitulation after stating I would never do it, made me look weak and stupid. Of course a much stronger reaction than this personal confession was about to take place and there can be little doubt that it was the tea break scenario that triggered a reawakening in my resentment and anger, but this time I had no conscious part in its appearance. It was as though I had within me a reserve of autonomous anger, independently acting out on my behalf, and indeed in this example I did perceive the emotion of anger before any intrusive thoughts began. Accepting this insight, it is then equally obvious that the thoughts that followed were derived from and were expressions of that anger and indeed their very nature proves that.

As the reader will be well aware by now, a large percentage of my symptoms were in the form of violent intrusive thoughts, were all these associated with this independent source of anger...? Well yes, I was to eventually discover they were, and what's more, the infantile way this anger was expressed revealed its long-standing origins. But it would be wrong to assume this internal generator of unbidden thoughts consisted of just raw emotion, for I have already described that it had a definite disposition to always do the opposite to my consciously held concerns and convictions, and in the last example there were two instances where interaction took place between this aspect and my normal thinking to produce more complex and specific intrusive ideas.

The first one occurred on the second return of the intrusive thoughts, there was an escalation in the violent form they took, namely the frightening idea of running amok. This is linked to my fears of losing control and going mad that had dominated my thinking during the first episode, I had this personal fantasy of the mad axe man beyond control and it was this that fuelled my fears and in opposite form fed the intrusive idea; in short, I feared it happening and therefore my internal generator showed it occurring.

The second example was an even quicker response to a conscious reflection, when the direct impulse to go and harm my boss appeared; I gratefully dismissed it by considering he was too far away to be in danger. Immediately the idea to harm him modified itself to negate this obstacle and now contained the impulse to jump into my car and drive to his office first. The connection here is self-evident; my attempt to mitigate the original impulse is used against me as it becomes an integral part of the intrusive thinking itself. These two illustrations alone tend to show that this other aspect of me although driven by anger, was capable of interacting with other mental processes and reacting to these in a manner reflecting its disposition.

I now move on to yet another distinct group of symptoms, one in which the super timid and fearful part of me appeared to play the major part; these intrusive thoughts are of a type I have come to know as my 'paranoid obsessions'. Why this label, well firstly because they are undeniably paranoid in nature, with their feelings and provoking thoughts about people and situations being hostile or somehow against me, and secondly I use the term obsession to distinguish them from true paranoid delusions, the difference being I'm critical and rejecting of my sudden paranoid ideas, in short I don't believe them, nevertheless like all obsessions they are hard to dismiss and are anxiety provoking. What follows next are some clear examples of this type of pathological thinking, all were originally recorded in my 1985 psychological diary. The first one only a short note really describes the sudden appearance of vulnerable and panicky feelings, often these were so strong that they had the power to taint one's perception of reality and immerse the adult in childlike feelings. On this particular Wednesday evening I had popped in to see my parents, all was initially fine... then suddenly I felt uneasy about myself, a feeling that quickly turned into outright anxiousness. Minutes later the usual thoughts of violence began along with strong fears of them, later as I crossed the road to go home (by 1985 I was married and living opposite) I became aware that the subject of the fear had changed; it was now focused on me being alone in a big world, I felt afraid and vulnerable in general and felt as if other people were somehow against me. The next day these ideas were still present and with it them continued the awful feelings of vulnerability and fear, despite the fact that I knew quite well that there was nothing in particular to be scared of. Later that day the fears became more explicit and spontaneously an emotionally charged memory of me alone and afraid in the school playground emerged. Had this memory even before I was aware of it, influenced the way I felt at a conscious level, after all at school the timid and vulnerable me had been scared of all those around me... it seemed my past fears were contaminating my present. The next example provides an even clearer illustration of this; it's a Saturday in April when I walk down to a local electronics shop to buy some components for some project I'm building, since gaining my HNC in electronics this is quite a common event. Once in the shop, which was quite small and this day unusually crowed I came face to face with two tough looking young men both dressed in motorcycle leathers. I was instantly afraid of them and with head down so as not to catch their eye I kept as far from them as possible. But on leaving the shop I had to edge past them and on doing so I just brushed against one, now sensibly I realized he hadn't even felt my touch, even so I glanced back to check and it was obvious that neither of them had noticed me. However as soon as I left the shop a constant nagging doubt appeared, the essence of which was that these two young men were following me. This intruding idea provoked an urge to continuously look round and check but this I resisted, knowing that the whole idea was unfounded and ridiculous. Now experiencing this particular symptom didn't cause me much anxiety in regard to it threatening my sanity, because I immediately recognised it as a reactivation of an old fear that had first appeared years before at school, therefore these two 'intimidating' men had merely awoken a fear system from a time when I felt particularly vulnerable trapped in the playground with such others. It is interesting to note that the compulsive act in response to the intrusion, namely the urge to turn to check could be suppressed... with difficulty yes, but nevertheless I could resist it, because the compulsive response is contrived and maintained within one's consciousness and thus one retains the power to have a corrective influence on it. This is in stark contrast to the intrusive material itself, which is just thrust upon one's awareness ready formed as it were, there has not been at a conscious level at least any involvement in its production, therefore insight is lacking and the power to influence or certainly to suppress its emergence is absent.

In the afternoon of the same day I was back at home and while sitting quietly I could plainly hear the roar of the crowd at the nearby football ground. Quite freely I imagined in the form of a daydream such a group of people all equally het up, against and after one person, and I pictured how terrifying this would be. At once an intrusive thought occurred suggesting that this imaginary person was I, the thought brought with it an intense fear of legitimacy, as if this was all really happening. More fear still was generated by my conscious reaction to the nature of these ideas, surely this was madness... paranoia like this must mean I was becoming psychotic. Panic welled up as I put it to myself that if I happened to believe these crazy ideas and acted on them I would be truly mad, but of course here lies the difference between psychotic and let's use an old here term neurotic conditions... at a fundamental level I didn't believe these ideas, nevertheless I was terrified that I might. The intrusive thoughts seemed once again to pick up and feed upon my fears and soon intruding mental images occurred compelling me to 'imagine seeing' groups of people waiting outside for me, almost as if to increase the paranoid fears. This in turn of course triggered my fears of hallucinations, what if I really believed I could see these people, thus more panic followed. What had begun as thoughts representing an intensely fearful and vulnerable aspect of me had in turn triggered consciously held fears about being mad, fears, which of course had their origins in my childhood dread of illness in general. But another element was also present an antagonistic aspect that appeared to play on the fears and compound and escalate the problem. All these different aspects played their part in the formation and maintenance of the symptoms that tormented me that day… how complex and hard to fathom was this bizarre and yet curious inner conflict. Nonetheless I was to ultimately discover that an understanding of all these underlying factors was possible and once achieved the nature of the symptoms themselves became comprehensible, to that very important insight I will return later. Continuing here I have another example of my paranoid obsessions and one that illustrates well how such intrusive ideas and doubts can affect one's relationship with important others.

According to my notes this event took place one Sunday in July 1987, after a day out my wife and I had returned home in the evening, for quickness and convenience my wife suggested we should have some frozen chicken nuggets for tea. Believing we hadn't bought these while shopping the day before, I asked her when we had got them, to which she replied in what seemed to me a flippant way, oh, only yesterday. There was something about this reply that got me thinking it was untruthful; I already knew from experience that she hated throwing food away. Nevertheless, I thought no more of it until the food was ready and we were sitting at the table, at which point my wife suddenly announced she didn't want any of the chicken and thus I could have it all. As I began to eat an intrusive doubt forced itself upon my awareness, it was in the form of a sudden intrusive conviction that the food was indeed old and probably bad as well. To make matters worse, along with this 'conviction', there appeared an emotionally charged idea implying my wife knew this, which of course explained why she wasn't having any. These thoughts once again possessed the usual obsessional insistence and uncanny self-importance so characteristic of this type of intrusion. My response was just as predictable as I almost automatically began to argue with and reproach myself for having such ridiculous and irrational ideas. At the same a wave of anxiety swept through me as my old fears of madness were activated once again. Despite all this I managed to fend off my fears and the level of anxiety dropped within a few minutes, even so a sort of residual doubt remained with me until later in the evening, my wife openly showed her love and affection for me. This emotional display seemed to reassure me at a fundamental level and the lingering unfounded suspicions disappeared.

So what were the triggers that called forth these particular intrusions, these paranoid type obsessions, as I like to call them. Well the seeds of doubt were plainly sown in the two exchanges with my wife concerning the

93

chicken. The first of these being the dismissive reply to my inquiry asking when it was bought, and the second her rejection of the food a few minutes later; both of these produced in me a moment of conscious considered 'wondering' but these doubts I easily managed to dismiss, only to have them reaffirmed in the content of the intrusive thoughts that followed. Obviously my internal generator of unbidden thoughts in this case my extremely fearful and timid aspect, reacted to these same triggers and maybe to my conscious doubts too. The affect was a much stronger mistrustful and suspicious reaction than I had, had at an adult level and it was these feelings that were the source of the resulting intrusive ideas. As I came to understand more of this fearful child aspect, I was to learn that he in fact didn't trust anyone. That's why his nature was that of a timid pleaser, over concerned how others felt and terrified of any sign of rejection. Of course in everyday life beneath the adult relationship, my wife was also subject to the propensities of this child like character, an important feature of which was that he didn't trust her either and was thus constantly looking for reassurance and proof that she did unreservedly love him/us, hence the profound effect when she was openly loving towards me later that evening. But my wife, in common with a number of other significant individuals, was not the original recipient of these feelings that individual I discovered later (via analysis) was my mother. Yes, I didn't trust my mother... did she love me unconditionally or only if I were her special good little boy who didn't have the mad eyes of father and grandfather? One good example of this doubt working away beyond my awareness was the compulsions that flared up when my brother was born (see chapter one). These, all relating to my mother, emanated from an inner fear of rejection or in this particular case of replacement... it was an event that confirmed of my badness. Thus the resulting compulsions were all about being extra good and nice, to prove I was still Mother's special little boy.

Sometimes symptoms were an even more obvious mix of the two autonomous tendencies within me and there is no better example of this than when intrusive thoughts appear in order to negate my own compulsive checking. Now compulsive checking in me ranged from the making sure I hadn't really hurt anyone already mentioned, to the more mundane and typically OCD checking of gas taps, light switches and water taps etc. This need to monitor and check originates from my anxious, fearful child aspect, I know this because when he is active all my compulsions increase dramatically both in what is included and length of time needed to try and find reassurance. Now when I'm in the middle of such compulsive actions, for instance making sure all the gas taps on the hob are absolutely off, which often involves trying the control knobs again and again and even smelling for gas; it is not unusual to have sudden intrusive images showing me/ urging me to turn on the very gas taps I'm taking so much trouble over making sure they're off. When this occurs an agony of indecision results as every check is nullify by a thought reversing that action, although in me the checking element tends to win out eventually. Another related example is what happens if I'm working with small and sharp objects such as drawing pins, nails or needles, or indeed if I break a glass resulting in sharp bits, I immediately have a nonsensical fear I might swallow some and thus need to go into hospital, the old fear resurrected once again. In such circumstances intrusive thoughts frequently occur urging me to throw the sharp objects into my mouth, a truly direct and opposite impulse to the fear that triggered it.

The very last description of a symptom in this chapter shows yet another side to my ever evolving and changing intrusive thoughts, this particular intrusion occurred on the 27th-April-1982 and because of its nature it was the first time I was able to discern a sort of rationale behind a symptom and also link it spontaneously to the external situation at the time. But for the reader to appreciate this I must once again set the scene and describe the circumstances. By this date I was the electrical/ deputy engineer at a small private hospital in Harrow sounds good doesn't it, but in reality we were only a small team, consisting of the chief engineer, myself and three others. One of these, a man called Ted who was the maintenance fitter was to become quite unjustifiably and all without his slightest awareness very important to me. Initially he wasn't of significance at all, we were just workmates and we got on ok together, the trigger event that was to change all that happened in mid 1981, when I announced to him that I was thinking of leaving. From that time on Ted showed a great deal more interest in what I did and asked a lot more questions about the controls, the boilers etc. than he had ever done before. Of course he was trying to find out as much as possible in case I did indeed leave... and leave him in the lurch so to speak, and at a rational level I knew and understood that. But his apparent sudden interest also evoked something far deeper than that, for overnight he became a sort of rival, I became jealous of him and felt that I was in competition with him for the acknowledgment of the chief engineer. In theory being the deputy I was the interface between the others and the chief, but I began to get a sort of intrusive doubt that Ted was going directly to him. This especially occurred if he walked past the workshop door (he had a distinctive step) rather than coming in, if this occurred I would get an intrusive idea he was going to discuss something with the chief engineer as his office was the next door along. Of course this is yet another example of my paranoid obsessions there was no foundation at all for any of this in reality and this I recognized at the time. So once again I became very anxious because of the 'madness' of it all in general, and because of the content of some associated intrusive thoughts, which were very angry as well as paranoid. The following copy of a note written in Sept 1982 indicates well what I was experiencing and how I felt about it:

The terrible hatred and jealousy has started again on Ted. The feelings are so strong and so out of proportion to my real feelings about him. Sometimes I feel this hate in me directly as I do today (the hate and the jealousy), most of the time I feel these only in my symptoms. With Ted it is as if I am in contest with him, trying to be better than him, or more importantly to be seen to be better than him.

It was in this self-generated atmosphere of mistrust and rivalry that the particular intrusion I wish to describe occurred, on that April day in 1982. This is how the event was recorded in my notes then: on Tuesday I was in the workshop when one of the men who works under me, Ted, came in and said the compressor had broken down. I at once said I knew what the problem was and that I would go and rectify it right away. I fixed the machine very quickly and I thought to myself I will try and catch Ted if he is still in the workshop and tell him it's now working. At that very moment my mind was filled with a rush different intrusive ideas and images, most showing me running about, rushing around and pushing things over. But at the same instant I seemed to perceive the meaning of the thoughts, they were this time self-evident being just a more extreme version of what I at adult level also wanted to do, namely catch Ted and inform him I had fixed the problem. But to the generator of my intrusive thinking I wasn't going fast enough and thus we might miss him, therefore in a childish equivalent to the adult wish the images showed me rushing to get there pushing things over if necessary, it was that important to tell Ted how clever and wonderful I had been. What could explain this duality within me, on the one hand a perfectly normal everyday relationship with a man I worked with, while on the other a childish rivalry and jealousy so strong and pervasive, that it endowed the ordinary working relationship between a colleague, the chief engineer and myself with enough emotion significance to resemble a close family unit... which of course it was... to the childlike source of the paranoid obsessions. My past (locked away within this childlike aspect) was influencing the way I perceived my present, in other words Ted and the chief were being treated as if they were significant people from my past, and as such they were cast to play a part belonging to that past. Now look away all those who don't like psychodynamic theory, for it is obvious to me now that Ted my workmate to the adult me had become my brother to the childlike me, while the chief engineer was father or indeed even mother. Appreciating this different level of functioning makes the rivalry, jealousy and need to be seen to be better than Ted, comprehensible, for it is nothing more than a small child's jealousy of a sibling, while trying to attract and maintain the attention of a parent. I personally feel there is no other explanation possible that would so adequately account for the disturbing and yet intriguing obsessions that were to plague my working life at the hospital.

In summary, I hope this chapter has demonstrated to the reader how my intrusive thinking once present, continued to interact with my internal and external life and by this process became progressively more complex in nature, while at the same time infiltrating more and more areas of my life. Because of this tendency for the symptoms to continually develop over time I have come to regard their first appearances as their purest and simplest form, and thus the easiest to understand. Considering this, it should be remembered that the angry oppositional aspect of me produced initially intrusions that were only in the form of punching and later some kicking. There was no use of weapons or any other addition or complication... there was only the sudden impulses to punch or kick in certain situations, a childlike response to threat I think most will agree.

It was only when I at a conscious adult level, began to fear this aspect of myself due to its apparent nature that other situations were added to the potentially dangerous list and certain everyday objects became potential weapons. It seemed that it was my very fears of what this angry aspect within me might do, that instigated what it did indeed want to do, within the content of the developing obsessional ideas. As I have mentioned before this part of me is characterised by being always being in opposition to almost every aspect of my normal functioning and to that of my fearful child element as well. It is as if this part is intrinsically negative and hostile towards the rest of my personality, consequently if I fear something then an intrusive thought will appear urging and showing me doing it. If I love or need something then intrusive ideas will show mental images of me breaking and destroying it and if I am relieved by something a memory or an occurrence for example, then invariably intrusive thinking will contrive something that spoils or negates it. It doesn't matter what I do... I cannot seem to change this aspect's response to the rest of me, no amount of rational argument, pleading or coercion makes any difference... he is what he is, and that is angry and oppositional by nature.

But it is apparent from the text that it wasn't just the angry and violent intrusions that developed and diversified, the ones relating to my fearful, timid child also changed. In certain circumstances this aspect of me if sensitive in some way to that event, acted autonomously reflecting its own disposition, the result could be a communication to the adult me of feelings of fear, guilt and concern, often associated with these emotions was a need for compulsive checking and monitoring of some kind. It is if this part of me is anxious vigilant, constantly watching the world and other people for signs of danger or rejection. The trouble is this fearful child aspect now resides within an adult personality consequently the range of experience and material it is subjected to, is vastly different from that normally available to a small child's mind. Hence this still active part from my past, has much more to interact with and be frightened of... for example if active (or he is close which is how I like to describe it) watching say a horror film frequently produces two reactions, an adult one, which may be enjoyment or indifference and a childlike reaction, which is much more strongly felt, consisting of real fear and concern mixed with a tendency to believe however far-fetched the films images are. Often it is this type of simple occurrence that best reveals the presence and persistence of childlike thought patterns within the adult while also providing insight into one cause of duality and conflict within a personality... for the average adult view is obviously at odds with the fear and irrational beliefs evoked within the child aspect. In the film example general insight and appreciating what the triggering material was, is not difficult. But as have I described in this chapter, the same underlying phenomenon can, I believe, be responsible for far more complex and intriguing conflicts ... conflicts which then become the source of equally elaborate symptoms.

Chapter Five

Know Thyself

On the 1st of April 1982 I attended my first session of Psychoanalysis with Dr Cutner at her home in Golders Green. I should say my first session of Analytical therapy really because Dr Cutner was predominantly a Jungian analyst, although she used in her actual therapy an eclectic mix of different schools of thought and techniques.

Already in her late seventies we had first met the week before in a sort of interview to see if I was suitable for analysis; her age and obvious wealth of knowledge seemed to make her a paragon of wisdom and one felt that whatever you said she had heard it all before. After some descriptions of my various symptoms, I told her I wanted to understand why I was like this... why did I play these awful 'games' within myself. She took notes, asked me about my past, my childhood, and sitting there as would become very familiar to me in the years to come; she acknowledged all I said in a calm and methodical way.

The large bookcase full of books just behind her seemed to emphasize her authority. On the small table beside her rested her all-important cigarettes and to the right were the French doors, which on a nice day would always be open to the garden beyond. Of course what she was doing during that initial interview after forming a conclusion about my mental state, which probably took her all of two minutes, was ascertaining whether or not I was suitable for analytical work… was I up to it, or even intelligent enough. Well I obviously passed, for by the end of the meeting I was being told what she expected from patients. You had to work with her, it wasn't just one way, hence there was homework, which consisted of writing up what had been discussed during the last session and noting any other significant occurrences between the sessions, plus of course recording any dreams.

Thus on the 1st of April I started my analysis, I had chosen Golders Green as this was the nearest location an analyst was available and it would take about 45 minutes to get there from home or work, an important consideration because I knew I would be going for some considerable time. Although at that stage I never envisaged I would be seeing Dr Cutner initially twice a week and then once a week for a total of five and a half years, in fact until she died suddenly in October 1987.

Now this isn't a book about having Psychoanalysis – that would require another book dedicated to that alone to do it any justice. But here I will relate of two little instances I remember well that show just a snippet of the interplay between patient and doctor is this special relationship. A lot of sufferers of OCD will I'm sure be able to identify with periods when the fear of one's intrusive thoughts gets out of hand, you fear they will get the better of you, resulting in one being forced against one's will to act them out. It is a dreadful feeling being terrified of oneself, for try as you might you cannot escape yourself, high anxiety and indeed outright panic occurs as one continually monitors the possibility the 'criminal within' might win out. I was in such a state at one session early on in my treatment and as we finishing up I gave the usual statement, that perhaps it would be better if I were locked up, rather than being a danger to others. Dr Cutner listened and nodded and then sat back for just a moment, calm and unperturbed, before replying with, obsessionals like you... for that's what you are, are pretty tough... I think you'll be all right! Doesn't sound much I know... but it was the way she said it that had the required effect, her knowing words seemed to burst the bubble of my unjustified terror. Plus of course I got a diagnosis and Dr Cutner was never fond of labels and I don't think I would have got one even then unless I was panicking. In analysis a certain amount of anxiety is tolerated and even fostered, for it motivates the individual to continue working and it also serves as a useful internal indicator that the material being dealt with or approached, is of importance or relevance.

The other little interaction of interest between the doctor and I concerned another common fear of many OCD sufferers, namely the inner fearful question are my symptoms an indication of madness. This doubt often occurred in me when any new type of symptom took hold especially if it seemed to challenge my preconceived ideas and rational thinking... my 'paranoid obsessions' were a good example of this. One session, again early on in my analysis I voiced this very fear by asking, what would happen if I did go mad? Again Dr Cutner sat back for a moment to ponder my question; a light breeze came in through the French doors momentarily lifting the net curtains so that the red, white and yellow roses in the garden could be plainly seen... then came the answer she quite simply said, then you would know your own unconscious... and that was it. Now of course in the context of analysis that is it, for the whole process is about illuminating and understanding aspects of oneself previously unknown. No mention of overwhelming emotions here, or of delusions and hallucinations, only the prospect of a profound inner journey. A journey in which I may indeed experience the vast inner universe of my psyche or at least an aspect of it, unfortunately such a confrontation would most probably leave me hopelessly psychotic... little chance for me the understanding and integration that Jung is said to have achieved in his own encounter with psychoses. Even so this alternative picture of madness even if very abstract seemed to allay my fears, the vast hinterland of the unconscious now seemed quite attractive within the context of the therapeutic journey I had now embarked on. Of course I was at the same time safe in the knowledge my analyst didn't believe I was mad nor was in any danger of becoming so. In fact, she gave this opinion a number of times during the course of my treatment, often with a little almost inner smile at my groundless fears, and she was also in a good position to judge for behind her lay years of experience of working with those with schizophrenia and other psychotic disorders. She even had a schizophrenic patient in analysis for two years and believed she was getting somewhere with him until time constraints forced her to cease contact. She believed that for this patient the schizophrenia represented (the psychogenic aspect of the disorder at least) a sort of failed personal philosophy, and the symptoms were in a way attempts by the individual to try to understand his experiences and the nature of his existence... those were the days, you'd just get a antipsychotic now.

So what had finally led me to seek treatment, after all by 1982 I had had OCD that is the intrusive thoughts opposite to my nature (ego-alien symptoms) for ten years, and the other fear driven symptoms etc. since the age of seven, marking my OCD as the early onset type. Well by this time marriage was on the horizon and I just couldn't marry someone without first informing them just what went on in my mind.

So one evening in 1981 I told my wife to be I had thoughts I couldn't control; she seemed to take it quite well really although that was probably so because I didn't go into much detail of what type of thoughts they were, even so she did insist I obtained some form of psychological help. At the time I had not used any form of label when describing my problems, but if I pressed I would have used the description Obsessive-Compulsive Neurosis (the term Obsessive-Compulsive Disorder & its abbreviation OCD was yet to appear) to best explain my symptoms. Since 1976 I had believed that this was what was wrong with me, this self-diagnosis occurred when out of fear I consulted a number of books on psychology, to see if they could explain what was happening to me. Luckily my symptoms were so plainly expressed that it was relatively easy to see close similarities between that described in the textbooks and my own experiences, and indeed my self-diagnosis has since been confirmed by two experts. Anyway motivated by my fiancée's concerns and harbouring a doubt I should have done something long before, I sought treatment for my condition. In December 1981 I found a therapist conveniently near to me so I could go direct from work from the hospital, he was a behaviourist who also used hypnosis. In hindsight he wasn't a good choice for I wanted to explore my symptoms and he didn't after the initial discussion, for his approach was one of removing the symptoms… not trying to understand them. Worse still I had, though I didn't know this at the time a phantasy concerning being influenced, (this belongs to my fearful child aspect) which of course hypnosis is associated with. I attended seven sessions in all during which time my symptoms got progressively worse, during hypnosis when I was meant to be relaxed I felt anxious and this was soon followed by intrusive thoughts of jumping up etc. Plus, the talking about my intrusive ideas, which continued despite my therapist's best intentions, seemed to increase my fear of them, especially the aggressive ones. The truth was, by now my OCD, and this is no reflection upon this particular therapist, was just too complex and intractable to be effectively dealt with by an approach that was basically superficial tinkering with its outer edges.

When later in February 1982 I received notification that this therapist had become ill and couldn't continue with his clients for sometime, I was unconcerned at the prospect of not going back. But the whole episode had left me much more concerned and anxious towards my angry and aggressive intrusive thoughts, which of course seemed to meet my fears by becoming more frequent and even more aggressive.

The breaking point came a few weeks later when I became physically ill (just a bug that was going round at the time) during which the idea struck me that in such a weakened state my intrusive ideas could overwhelm me, at once my level of anxiety rose considerably, and on the verge of panic I monitored myself continuously while unbidden thoughts gave me hell on earth. I was in this anxious and vulnerable state when I first called on Dr Cutner for that interview late in March; I needed help so I was up for any amount of homework she demanded.

Analysis and the support offered within such a special relationship presents many opportunities beyond just the understanding and perhaps the resolution of a psychological disorder. It is in a way another chance to grow, a new possibility to mature while diminishing those elements of one's past that predisposed the personality to later disturbance. But for me the most important outcome was that it provided the approach, the tools and the courage to look at my symptoms in a new way, and not just to try and run from them and be grateful when they disappeared. From that time on I noted where and when intrusive ideas occurred, I began to see how similar events would evoke a particular thought or compulsion and eventually I perceived themes returning again and again, representing certain sensitivities within my personality. Well beyond my time in analysis... well for the next 30 years really I was to continue to use the technique of 'purposeful introspection' on my symptoms and on me in general, in an attempt to finally understand the mental processes that took place beyond my ken, but yet affected my life so profoundly. Be sure of this though OCD is no easy adversary it is a very complex and multifaceted disorder with its roots deep in one's past and the triggers in one's present. It is as if aspects of oneself following their own propensities intrude upon and disrupt the main adult personality, which luckily is strong enough to hold out and remain reality adjusted... in other words you don't go mad. But however complex and impenetrable the edifice of OCD seems, it will in my opinion eventually yield up its underlying structure, and become intelligible if it is studied long and hard enough. At the start of my analysis this was the journey I was about to embark on, it was initially incredibly difficult and slow going. For the first few weeks I felt I just wasn't getting anywhere, worse still my anxiety remained very high as the terror of my intrusive thoughts perhaps breaking through into reality haunted me every day. Then three months after I had started treatment there was a spontaneous development from within, which changed everything and was the beginning of my real journey into self-knowledge.

It was now July and the months of anxiety and accompanying periods of panic had taken a heavy toll on me, there was also a strange feeling of turmoil within my mind and this was steadily growing, something was going on within me but I didn't know what, nevertheless I did know I was completely at the mercy of it. Then in late July while at the hospital this extreme feeling of mental stress reached a crisis point, it seemed as if was a tight band around my head, a head which felt as if it was about to explode at any moment. I knew I had to get somewhere safe and away from others and luckily nobody ever missed the deputy engineer, so I quickly climbed the stairs to the roof and from there to the safety of the roof top plant room. Here alone with only the noise of the air-conditioning units for company I sort of yielded to whatever was happening to me; a sort of emotional upsurge began as a physical sensation in my stomach before it welled up into my throat and burst forth as sudden sobbing crying, a crying that didn't stop and which racked my whole body. In that same instant images, memories and accompanying emotions poured out of me… I felt like a young frightened child in a big world. An image of me standing alone in the playground occurred first, raw feelings of being lost and vulnerable followed. Then masses of mixed general feelings appeared almost too fast for me to record and the theme of these feelings was one person, namely Mother. Fears of her dying, fears of her leaving all mixed with a terrible dread and sadness, as each of these feelings appeared I seemed to experience them as real and new. The reactions and emotions of a child became mine again, the tears, the anguish of being separated from Mother flooded my mind and for fleeting moments seemed to displace the adult me. Then without apparent change to the young age of this inner image, the spontaneous thoughts moved on to when at the age of 13 I had felt rejected and ignored by my father. I now relived this period of my life, experiencing the hurt, the bitterness once again; strangely the feelings evoked struck me as being even stronger than my adult memories of this period. Within 30 minutes of starting this cascade of thoughts and emotions gradually abated and then stopped... I had my mind back. Although still in shock I felt a great deal better... gone was the anxiety and the strange inner turmoil, gone also was that immense feeling of pressure within my head. Somehow this sudden release of emotion with its associated images and thoughts had naturally brought relief to my inner suffering. Of course I was soon to discover that this was only a temporary respite the emotions would build up again and constrained by the same internal themes would appear again and again linked to the same images and thoughts. Curiously I was to discover that my angry and aggressive intrusions also diminished following such a spontaneous release, this occurring even though the emotional release itself contained no reference to such feelings. Thus it would seem that my internal angry aspect was somehow linked to the fearful child aspect. At an adult rational level I naturally recognised this vulnerable and fearful child image as a return of how I felt and indeed was, after leaving school at the age of 15... after 10 years of only indirect expression this part of me was back.

The following examples are a record of the thoughts and feelings that spontaneously appeared during these emotional releases, although not all episodes were as intense as that described above. For it seemed that once the aspect had found expression it could continue to communicate unsolicited feelings and thoughts to me without the dramatic 'breaking through' of the initial event... although emotionally intense episodes did also continue. In order to assist the reader's understanding additional notes or words added now are enclosed in brackets thus [...]. It will be noticed that the examples used are not necessarily in chronological order, (this being especially true in later chapters) for I have mostly chosen content over strict sequential order, where this I feel would be more informative to the reader; also the same diary entry may appear more than once for the same reason. Furthermore, expect repetition of theme across the various diary entries, after all consistency of theme over the years is how I came to know and understand my inner world, and this I wish to convey to the reader.

31st July 1982:
Can't grow up, need mother... terrible fear
Fear of the world, fear of growing old, fear of leaving Mummy, fear of being on my own.
Fear of time passing, of growing old, getting old... growing up, growing up!
Fear, fear, fear... fear of becoming separate from my mother, fears of being alone, lost... fears!

8th August 82:
[an example of feelings only, i.e. no thoughts or images]
Feelings of fear all day, feel so insecure like a small child... terrible feelings of sadness for my past life.

12th August 82:

I don't want to grow up, I don't want to, Mummy's going now... say goodbye, no, no, no!
I am aware of a small child crying bitterly as I want to cry for him, frightened of being bad in Mummy's eyes.
Mummy might die, can't leave her... she might die.
I can't grow up without Mummy... leave me alone; leave me *[in communication these other aspects of me seemed to regard adult me as an external person]*.
She might die; she'd be on her own.
Don't want to leave home because of Mummy. Mummy's not safe!

[Later same day]
Mummy what about Mummy!
Don't want to get older; don't want to grow up.
What about Mummy: Mummy may die if I leave.
Mummy will be so upset if I leave her, Mummy needs me. Mummy might die and leave me.

25th August 82:
Hospitals, illness, punishment! *[Remembering the powerful associations with these in my childhood]*.
Why me? I hate myself, I do... I hate Mummy.
Why? *[Spontaneous question appearing with the general flow of thoughts, i.e. not me the adult asking]*. She hates me.
You'll have to go to the hospital to see what's wrong with you. Couldn't trust Mummy.

[Later same day]

Fear of loneliness; fear of being alone.

Mummy, Mummy, where's my mummy.

Fear of being left alone... left alone, left alone.

Fear of strangers'... fear of being rejected.

Lost, fear, lost... to be loved, needed.

Run home be with Mummy for protection.

Everybody turning against me... Mummy doesn't love you any more, why! *[Spontaneous question]* I don't know [why] I don't care... I do, I do!

The fear of people turning against me, even Mother.

Fear of the world... fear of losing Mother.

The fear of people turning against me... even Mother.

[Later same day]

Alone in the world, all-alone in the world... who will protect me.

Who's going to look after me, no Mummy?

Such a lost little boy, alone and frightened... what can he do *[a feeling perception that appeared with the thoughts]*.

1st September 82:

Loneliness, fear of being alone... *Mummy, Mummy where are you, dead?*

Fear of being left alone, growing old, of leaving people.

Fear of Mummy dying, being alone, alone [I'm] frightened.

Terrible dread of people I know dying... fear of being separated forever and nothing can be done about growing old, growing up.

Growing, dying, separating... leaving the past behind, living and dying.

The terrible sadness of separation, of leaving, of going.

People dying, I can see Mother, Father dying as if the fear of death touched me early on *[an adult interpretation of a feeling perception that appeared with the thoughts]*.

As if I'm compelled to think of the last separation... being alone.

To grow up [I] can't, no, no... why? *[Spontaneous question followed by the answer]* Mother will die when you grow up.

[Later same day]

Terrible dread of people dying, [of] being left alone in the world.

Something here a terrible [feeling] of loss... not wanting to grow up and face these things, becoming old, growing up... a terrible dread.

A terrible fear of dying coming up now [perception of the mood before the associated thoughts begin].

The final leaving, parting... leaving people:

Don't leave me!

Don't leave me!

Why, why!

[Later same day]

It is as if there was a terrible sadness in me... wanting to, ready to come out *[adult reflection on how I felt].* Everything seems so uncertain as if a feeling of doom hangs over me. Keep coming back to memories at about [the age of] six, as if I can't face the final separation...[the] fear! *[This refers to adult held memories of as a child crying while frightening myself with thoughts that my parents might die].*

These examples should, I feel, be adequate for the reader to appreciate the nature of these spontaneous thoughts, there were many others from this period I could have used, but the same themes are merely repeated. The themes themselves are plainly discernible and here I identify five:

a) A profound fear of growing up also referred to in the notes as moving on and getting old. The most important consequence of this growing up seemingly being Mother dying, growing old or being left alone.

b) Related to the above, a fear of becoming or being separate from Mother, also referred to as being alone, lost or leaving Mummy and often in other notes as the last goodbye.

c) Mother is deemed to be not safe; hence I must stay with her.

d) Despite the obvious attachment and dependence upon Mother, there is anger and hate directed at her.

e) There is a marked distrust of others apparent, shown clearly in the remark, people turning against me... even Mother.

From the content of the above rush of thoughts I believe it is self-evident that the source must be a childlike aspect still active within the adult me. The fact that the fears and concerns represented in these thoughts were in essence the same that dominated my childhood supports this view... the fearful child of my past was back. During this period the emotions/ feelings of a child touched upon above stayed with me on a continuous basis, although they were additionally heightened during the duration of the spontaneous thought 'attacks'. Hence I felt afraid, vulnerable and small in a big world etc., but in addition to this I became super sensitive, nostalgic and over sentimental, these feelings being so powerful that they were literally painful to experience. In particular, while in this state I became extremely altruistic, full of compassion and concern for anyone or anything that was: lost, alone, afraid, hurt/ broken, or dying etc., notice here my concern was not only for people or animals but for objects too. It would seem that this child aspect's compassion, was equally evoked by misfortune to inanimate items as well, and indeed the emotional reaction was just as raw, especially if the object was for example a human or animal shaped toy. Another obvious divergence from my normal adult view was my morality changed during this period. In other words, I felt very guilty about things that normally wouldn't bother me and if I infringed any of these 'new' rules I had a most unpleasant feeling I would get punished in some undefined way... any reader who has read chapter one should not be surprised at this particular returned tendency. Associated with this increased guilt was a sort of anxious sensitivity in regard to other people, the slightest verbal or usually non-verbal indication that I had upset someone, filled me with instant fear and guilt, I had become a committed pleaser again due to inner fears of rejection.

But what was happening to me during this period of spontaneous thoughts and powerful emotions, what would explain the way I felt, which was so different and at odds with my normal everyday personality. Well from the very first I instinctively recognised the material as a return of childish thinking and feeling, in fact the emotional release that occurred in that hospital plant room thirty odd years ago, was the first real piece of personal insight of my analysis. Years later and after a number of these returns (return of the child) as I came to know them, I became familiar with both the triggers and stressors that precipitated them, and of the content of the material so liberated; which was virtually always the same, the themes only slowly changing as interaction took place between these aspects and the rest of my mental functioning. But by what mechanism did I experience these other parts of me, it would be easy just to say they were separate sub-personalities within my main adult personality, for I certainly experienced them as such, that is, they appeared to be mini autonomous personalities following their own agenda in my mind. Each one and the duality here is that alluded to throughout this story namely the fearful/ anxious child and his angry opposite, revealed itself as a complex (in the psychodynamic sense of the word) with its own identity, memories and cognitive ability, together with its own reserve of emotional energy, the nature of which reflected the disposition of that complex/ mini personality. But is how I perceived these other aspects in my mind a true and accurate representation of how they really are… the truth is I just don't know, I will merely state here something Dr Cutner once told me when we touched upon this very subject… she said of autonomous personalities 'they are an indication of the complexity of the human mind'. But what I do know from direct personal experience is that when these complexes were strongly active or close, I was much more disturbed with greatly increased OCD symptoms, increased anxiety and often a tendency towards panic attacks. In me these periods of heightened symptoms lasted around three or four months, before the anxiety would seem to naturally decrease and the symptoms would return to my 'normal' everyday level. These episodes as bad as they were to experience demonstrated to me that these inner active areas with their strange thoughts and raw emotions were even when not overtly active, the source of my regular intrusive thoughts and at least some of my compulsions.

121

There have been six such returns in total, all resulting in periods of heightened symptoms and in the years 93, 95 and 2010/11 totally incapacitating anxiety as well. Each had its own external or internal triggering event as described below:

a) 1972: Leaving school as discussed in chapter two.

b) 1982: Seeking treatment as mentioned in this chapter.

c) 1993: The collecting together and writing up of old notes concerning my disorder.

d) 1995: The chance seeing in a cemetery of a gravestone with 'Daddy and Mum' on it.

e) 2010/2011: Being ill with a heart problem (arrhythmia).

f) 2012/2013: Writing this book, plus the death of a pet.

In addition, the following evoked symptoms, which although not as intense as those above, were appreciably worse than my everyday symptomatology.

g) 2005: Being ill with stomach problems (probably an ulcer).

h) 2009: Fear of illness, due to my high blood pressure at the time.

Once the different triggering events have been set down like this, it's plain that they all represent aspects of life that my inner child complex was particularly sensitive too. Although there are two exceptions in 1993 and 2012/13 when merely rereading and copying down earlier notes concerning the above, was seemingly enough to evoke the material locked away in my complexes. In fact, in 1993 I was completely caught out by this phenomenon, when during a period of almost no troubling symptoms I decided to reorganize some of my old notes by copying them all into one book for safe keeping. Within a few weeks of starting this I became anxious for no apparent reason, then the violent intrusions and fear of them increased dramatically. Eventually this was followed by spontaneous crying linked with various fears and the need for Mother, along with this last aspect came a return of the strange paranoid obsessions... in short I became very ill for some months. One outcome of this new insight was that it provided additional proof that it was indeed these active autonomous areas that were the source of my pathological thinking... after all, the stirring up of these areas had beyond reasonable doubt resulted in an escalation in my symptoms. This was to happen again while writing this book, of course I was now more prepared for this possibility even so it did evoke an additional vulnerability in me and when our cat died the child complex promptly returned, producing typical symptoms for some weeks. I feel sure this would not have happened if it were not for this complex already being active due to my introspections and I would have experienced our pet's death only on an adult level.

123

The other triggers listed are more obviously external events to which there was a particular inner sensitivity, there is plainly at least one theme here that of being ill. If at any time I become ill especially if I didn't know the cause or it persisted, then there was not only adult concern present but also outright panic from my child. Anyone who has read chapter one should not be surprised at this reaction, for the fears of my childhood are of course represented and live on in the child complex. Another trigger apparent is anything to do with death, such as the chance seeing of the gravestone with daddy and mum on; this of course invoked fears of my parents dying, being alone and of the last goodbye. The death of our pet cat in 2013 had a similar effect but curiously with the feelings reversed as now my child complex was overwhelmed with concern for the cat, as being small and alone and frightened. The 1982 trigger that of seeking treatment, was effectively an external equivalent to my rereading my notes it had the same invoking and stirring up effect. The first major return triggered by leaving school and marked by my breakdown; evoked the inner fears of growing up, moving on and leaving Mother behind, so profound was the effect of this and the subsequent pushing back to work that it released the angry child aspect, who was to haunt the adult me from then on. To support what has been stated so far in this chapter, what follows are a number of different examples recorded over several years of how this inner child complex revealed itself to me, as usual all information is either from my psychological diaries or analysis notes. I start with some of the spontaneous outpouring of thoughts and feelings that occurred in 1993, it is interesting to compare this to the earlier example from 1982.

13th June to 15th June 93

Still active *[the child complex]* calling for mummy, frightened mummy will die... just frightened and the feeling of this.

[In the] morning, feeling anxious together with images of Greenhill school [my primary school in Harrow] the little boy feelings of leaving mummy, being alone. Also the feeling of not having much comes up, [i.e. perhaps] only a little toy or just a broken little gift, little cake etc. and nothing else.

My little [child complex] visited me today, much emotion, much crying. But not much insight into his feelings [of the] thoughts or memories that did come up the following: I want mummy, things breaking, pens, toys etc. and only having a broken little thing left and nothing else. I haven't got anything... lots of crying and sadness!

17th June & 20th August 93

He appears very quickly *[child complex]* crying, floods of tears and the same thoughts:

Mummy where are you... Mummy where are you!

Feeling I want Mother, where has Mother gone.

[The] feelings, anguish, fear... great fear!

There's a fear feeling that latches on to anything and causes [the adult me] anxiety. I fear my angry side even more now.

He is very upset [*child complex*] crying etc.:
Mummy, Mummy… I want Mummy.
I don't want to grow up… no!
[*Why? A self question from the observing adult me*] I don't want Mummy to grow old and die.
I get the feeling this child aspect of me is trying to keep the old times forever.
Don't leave me Mummy, don't leave me Mummy.
I remember the stories [of] mothers dying etc.

From the above it is obvious that the same concerns and fears first expressed in 1982 are once again the main themes here, although there are subtle differences, of which 'only having a broken little thing' is one example. Also I think it important to note here that the child of six who attended Greenhill School and indeed had his own fair share of fears and difficulties there, is not the child expressed via the spontaneous thoughts even though there is reference to the school. This is a much younger child aspect that was present, but not represented or even directly known about when the older me attended this school. A good example of this inner splitting or dissociation occurred when my brother was born, for this one event produced two distinct reactions. The first, the concern and wonder of an unsettled 10-year-old, while the second was a far younger response much more intense and fearful; this deep-seated reaction made itself know to the older me, via the compulsive actions I felt obliged to do, these expressed the younger aspect's need to show Mother he was still her good little boy. This requirement to be good and fear of being bad is a very common element in many of my notes, as is the term 'raw child' an expression I coined to describe this infantile aspect of me... because he was so emotionally painful to experience. The following are more illustrations of how this raw child made his present felt:

4th April 1995
My raw child told me today *[spontaneous thoughts]* that he is afraid of losing mummy by being bad, like a bad person, a wicked person... because then he would be all alone.

5th April 1995
My raw child has been very close to me this week, I'm glad because it reminds me of how bad [miserable & upset] this child feels. His fears were of people dying, being alone, being a bad [amoral] person, and such fears they are... I must not underestimate them!

17th April 1995
My raw child is very close to me this morning [there is] crying, the feeling of [a] loss that cannot be made up... of fear.

[Later]

some of the things I imagine like dying and leaving mummy behind, reminds me of what I used to imagine [while] in bed [when I was 6 years old] about my parents dying. There is also a mix of feelings, not having much and so on.

[Later]

a number of images came up all from my little raw child, who is still very close to me. [For example a] sudden feeling and image of [me] standing alone... feeling absolutely hopeless and crying/ wanting to cry, I felt as if I was in the playground [at Greenhill School]. [Next] while in the supermarket suddenly had an image of me, throwing something down and standing in utter despair and crying. [Also while] at Whitmore High School sudden feelings of wanting help [and] despair came over me; this seemed to remind me of my first lunchtime there, also associated with this [was] a bad feeling of not knowing what to do and [something] about my sandwiches.

Whitmore High had been Lascelles secondary modern for boys when I had attended there, hence the personal reaction. I could call on any of the schools I had attended in Harrow during this period (1987 to 2002) because I was now a council officer with the duty of checking on electrical work carried out in school premises. From the note concerning the high school it may be discerned that my young child aspect was also active while I was at secondary school hence the same feeling of vulnerability and fear and this is one example of many such intrusive feelings I experienced while in the school environment. The sandwiches are deemed important here because anything given to me my mother was regarded so, they appear in this next example also:

25th February 2011
Went to Kendal early it was a dark and wet day, soon after I got there I felt vulnerable and scared of people. Then I seemed to be seeing the wet ground in a different way... a memory was pushing its way into my mind, of a wet and dark morning going to school [I'm] full of fears for the day to come, wanting to run home... next the memory/ smell of egg sandwiches in foil. I feel as if I want to cry... difficult out in the street, but my raw child is already crying. [He] seems to remember holding them; touching them [the sandwiches] they are important because they are from home and Mother. While [he] in a dark corner of the playground... frightened. [Note concerning the above experience made at the time] the above reminds me of the theme in me of 'only having a little thing, but it being very important'. This must be something from home, something Mother has given to me and then when alone and frightened I hold it... it's important; it's a connection to Mother and safety. Thinking about this evokes the child again he is crying, he has been very close to me today as indeed he was yesterday... lots of crying today as I the adult have tried to comfort him.

129

The next two entries are other examples dealing with the same general theme:

14th July 1993

Morning, feeling of anxiety together with images of Greenhill School... leaving mummy, being alone. Also the feeling of not having much i.e. only a little toy or just a broken little gift, little cake etc. and nothing else!

27th September 1982

[The] food smell at the hospital at once reminded me of school; the wet ground [becomes] the playground. With these memories, the feelings of loneliness and wanting to run home to Mother.

As the reader will be fully aware of by now closely associated with the raw child was the angry child aspect. The following note from 2002 illustrates this connection extremely well.

4th July 2002

Today my little raw child was close to me; I felt his vulnerability and fear. Also while walking in Harrow one of [my] very first symptoms returned, [the intrusive thought] of punching people as I walked past them. So the situation is my raw child feels anxious and vulnerable, thus so do I because of the influence of his feelings... while Rebel wants to punch people.

Who is Rebel, I hear the reader quite justifiably say. Well this was the name I gave to my angry aspect, the generator of my unbidden violent thoughts, sometime during 1982. It is indeed a very suitable name for a part of me that appears to be in constant revolt against the rest of my personality. If I fear or recoil from something Rebel invariably wants to do it, he is the quintessential oppositional and negativistic child (complex) within me. Rest assured there will be much more about Rebel in the next chapter; meanwhile these notes from 2009 and 2011 demonstrate further the relationship between the fearful child and his angry opposite.

31st July 2009

No notes for a long time but now my raw child is back evoked by my fears of being ill. *[I had high blood pressure at the time]* One should never forget the emotional power of [this] child aspect. He is crying, frightened, alone and calling mummy, mummy, mummy! *[In later returns the intrusive calling of mummy was an accurate indication that my raw child complex was active, or was about to become so.]* Again associated with him is [the feeling] of only having a small, little object left [but this is so] important to the child. Also the feeling [which is hard to experience and endure] that no one can save him... [also] he can't trust anyone not Mother, [or] God etc. Of course Rebel is also present with the punching symptom.

131

6th September 2011

Today my raw child is very close to me, [consequently I'm] close to tears and I feel alone and vulnerable and there is the tendency to feel for others [beyond my normal concerns] plus there is the feeling of not having much… all this is very typical raw child stuff.

[Next] just after lunch sudden impulse to violence appears… a sort of general [intrusive] anger, this causes me some anxiety (as if I might act on it). Then very soon after lots of emotion from my raw child i.e. much crying and shouting mummy, mummy… he was suddenly so very close. What an exceedingly good example of the link between my fearful child and Rebel personality.

One more illustration I think of the general impact this child complex had on the adult me, before moving on to more specific areas of influence, often subtle due to the different facets of this inner child's character.

15th October 2011

My raw child has been very close to be me these few days, a consequence of studying my old notes. There's a lot of crying, feeling afraid/ vulnerable and sometimes [the feeling of] wanting to run home [my old childhood home that is]. Also the other paranoid, strange and fearful type thoughts have picked up again. When [he is] close anything slightly different from 'normal' or odd, especially if the adult me can't explain it straight away, seems to throw my raw child into panic. It is as if he

132

views the world with a constantly anxious eye... anything out of place, not as remembered, is a trigger causing panic and sometimes intrusive thinking.

Earlier in this chapter I stated the opinion that my child complex was still, even when not strongly active, the source of some of my spontaneous intrusions. The following example from 1991-93 of a very strange little obsession indeed, is a clear illustration of such symptom formation and offers some 'proof' that my raw child complex had a large part to play in its production.

1991

[During a period of few really troubling symptoms and consequently low anxiety.] One night while reading a book about snakes in bed, a particular black and white line drawing of a snakes' skin triggered a momentarily awareness of the superficial similarity to the skin on my hand that was holding the book. Interesting... so what, let's read on was my adult rational reaction, but at that same instant there came an internal stirring, in the form of a feeling of doubt, unknowing fear and concern all mixed up together and thrust compulsively upon my awareness. Then appeared a spontaneous intrusive thought and image of having a snake's head on my arm instead of a hand, yes that's right an arm ending in a snake's head...a crazy idea indeed I think most will agree, and indeed my conscious reaction to it was outright confusion and panic. In that moment my fears of madness and its consequences came

flooding back… after all was not this nonsensical thinking the very stuff of psychosis, for if I believed such an intrusion I would no doubt be mad. But how had it come about, once again the duality in me is striking, an adult rational view parallel to an irrational infantile one, which due to its compulsive nature seems to pull me away from my mature structured thinking. The trigger here of course had been the superficial similarity between the drawing and my skin; this had produced in addition to my ordinary adult acknowledgement, a young childlike response the conclusion of which was essentially… the substance of the pathological intrusion. It must be remembered that the thinking in very young children is very different to that of adults, and I would urge the reader to study this area of psychology. For an insight into infantile thinking processes provides an understanding of the origin and nature of the material, I believe lays behind many obsessions and compulsions. In this example the superficial similarity noted by the adult me produced in my child aspect the conviction they were the identical, because to the young child 'two objects that are similar are the same'… the child view 'makes no provision for chance', in addition the common-sense impossibility of this conclusion is not a consideration of the magical thinking child's mind. This event resulted in an obsession that was to persist for a few months although it was never a major source of anxiety after the initial panic; eventually it was displaced by other obsessions linked in turn to their intrusions, in that natural progression for me of pathological thinking running in parallel to my 'normal' everyday life.

Then approximately two years later in 1993 when I was experiencing one of my 'returns' as described earlier in this chapter, this return being the one triggered by my decision to collate my old notes. There occurred an intrusive thought that helped me to confirm the origin of this very strange idea. In the midst of the fear and anguish, the upsurge in symptoms and the strange irrational thinking, all typical of my child complex being particular active or close... there appeared during one very anxious day an absolutely spontaneous return of the image and idea of the snake hand. By absolutely spontaneous I mean it was completely out of the blue, there was no external triggers and at a conscious level I had forgotten all about this obsession and yet here it was once again... strongly individually represented, and yet wrapped up in a mass of other ideas and feelings I naturally recognized as my childlike aspect. This was proof for me... if proof can be said to be achievable in this type of psychological work, then this was it. The association between the obsession and this other aspect of me was clear, and indeed can be shown in other examples, some of which are included in the next chapter.

As mentioned, another consequence of the raw child's influence was that my sense of morality changed, I began to feel additionally guilty over everyday situations and obsessionally analyse any events where I felt I had done something wrong. The closer or more active my child complex, the stronger were these guilt feelings and their associated obsessive checking; the following three entries all from my diaries illustrate this. I was sometimes responsible during the time I was a council officer for disabled hoists, stair lifts etc. in the borough, hence my concern about such a hoist in this first example.

4th October 1995
Felt so guilty today… about not doing anything about the hoist *[sometimes it was very difficult to get decisive action in a situation where access was awkward or social services were involved]*. But [later] the guilt seemed totally out of proportion, I even had to return to work… I just had to *[that is return to the civic centre from being out on site, instead of going straight home]* to get the phone number [in order to check the situation]. This feeling now is so different from how I felt this morning at work; I must remember to listen to this other part of me. In fact, this feeling is the same (but stronger) as when I forgot to give the message to Dave *[a colleague]* i.e. intense guilt over nothing really… these guilt feelings I feel are very much associated with my raw child.

The above is a mild example compared with the following similar event also in 1995. The trigger this time was an illuminated street sign, which had its inspection panel missing. Now I had no responsibility for these at all, but I always felt I should report the smallest problem... basically my guilt ridden personality even feared that I may harm someone by omission and this resulted in me basically feeling over responsible for all those around me in potentially any situation.

29th April 1995

Yesterday I saw a street sign that needed reporting to street lighting, I don't like reporting these things... so I tried to put it off. At once I had that feeling of being absolutely bad and the [obsessional] thought, 'if you don't do this you will be so bad' [followed]. I think what is happening here was due to my raw child being so close/ active at the moment and so where I would normally have felt a little guilty I now feel this absolute guilt feeling. Both feelings come from the raw child, but this absolute feeling and fear of being bad, is at his very root.

The final example below reveals how even the most trivial event could trigger guilt and fear feelings within my child complex, all due to an everyday occurrence that normally would not have caused me any distress or concern at all.

February 2011

While driving, to help me relax I switch on the CD player the second song on the disc happens to be Golden Brown by the Stranglers, now I like the tune of this and I would have ordinarily listened to it quite happily without a second thought. But somewhere in my memory there is the recollection that the lyrics allude to the drug heroin. Because of this an adult held association, my raw child who is particularly close at the moment reacts, and the feelings of being bad spontaneously appear... that uncanny absolute conviction of being bad and a fear of the consequences. I find myself having to turn it off, there's no way my fearful, guilt ridden child can listen to this, to do so feels bad, so wicked... there is also a fear of contamination here i.e. becoming bad if I don't care and just continue listening. Once again a striking duality within me one part unconcerned and indifferent and the other intensely fearful of being corrupted, of being bad and fearful of the consequence.

The following two reflective notes written during the return of 2010/11 further illustrate my raw child's unforgiving morality and its impact on the adult me.

23rd February 2011
My raw child is afraid of God this is shown by the compulsions of my childhood e.g.
The praying obsession, the compulsive self- punishments to ward off God's punishment and the pervasive general fear of punishment if I did something I felt was wrong. These fears are I believe still alive and find expression in some of my adult intrusive ideas *[in other words the intrusive ideas I experience now]*.

1st April 2011

My raw child fears being bad… his morality is much more absolute than mine. Anything he considers wrong can't be done… there is a fear of punishment here, when my raw child is close as he is to me now, then all these feelings are much more intense… he is so very worried about being bad. All this is just like my *[guilt]* concerns from my childhood.

I have previously mentioned that my perception of the child aspect within me is as a separate autonomous personality. Indeed, I also have some awareness that this 'child' regards me in a similar manner i.e. as a separate person in regard to him, the following note from 2010 demonstrates this:

19th December 2010

I imagined that I the adult me had returned to Greenhill School to find my raw child alone in the playground, [the intention was symbolically] to take him back with me, to look after and take care of him. But on trying [to approach him] I had the very same [intrusive] thought I get for others… but now [it was directed at me so] I was bad or potentially bad, he drew back from me… note my raw child doesn't even trust me… I need to win his trust!

But what had shaped this child's personality and especially the pathological elements, which I now believe form the troubled bedrock of my OCD. Well this child has

139

known psychological traumas and on rare occurrences I too (the adult me) have glimpsed aspects of these when he the child has been very active or close. During these few instances I have experienced momentarily the content and nature of these traumatic episodes, and the raw emotions generated by them. Believe me confrontation with this level of terror and anguish is not for the faint-hearted and even before this depth of insight could occur, I had to be so close to my child complex that I was already quite 'ill' with greatly increased anxiety and the characteristic upsurge in all other symptoms. The following notes from 1995 and 2011 illustrate how I experienced two of my child aspect's traumatic memories; one event was consciously instigated, although I quickly lost control of what resulted while the other was completely spontaneous, occurring during a period when I was already very 'ill' indeed.

16th April 1995

[Today] did [therapeutic] work with my raw child, went back to Greenhill School to meet him and mummy by the small [entrance] gate. I asked if I could go in with him and took his hand, we said goodbye to mummy and went in at the old green gates we turned and said goodbye again. Then we walked about our old playground... right around to the toilets at the far end, here the bell went my raw child at once wanted to go back and see mummy before we had to go in and this we did and waved to her. Then the whistle went which meant we had to line up in our classes, we were at the end of the line I still held my child's hand... we could still see mummy, standing just outside the school. Then just as the line moved off [to go inside the school, and at this point I lost control of the contrived images] such emotion grabbed me, it was a powerful physical feeling within my body and stopped my breathing. A very powerful feeling indeed that suddenly turned into a sobbing cry, at that same moment I seemed to actually remember watching mummy when standing in line in the playground, I have never managed to remember any of this before.

[Later]
I seem to get an image of my raw child [at school] drying his eyes with a hankie mummy has given him.

The above episode relates to the period when I started at Greenhill School, then aged five and a bit this proved to be a very difficult transition for me, one that was necessitated by the family moving from Paddington to Harrow. Although I had already been at school for just over a year, the move to a new one where everyone had settled in, made friends etc. was deeply distressing to the timid, shy and passive little boy I was... a little boy who was no more than a façade of an even more insecure, mother fixed and fearful child. Curiously, I can't remember these early months at Greenhill in spite of having memories either side of it... it is lost to my adult repertoire of memories and yet, as the above shows it still exists and indeed appears to be part of my raw child complex... or at least this aspect of me has access to these memories, where I don't.

Therefore, much of what I do know comes from my mother's recollections and she readily admits it was a difficult time for us both. Now Mother who brought me to school each day, was of the habit of waiting by the gate (and she wasn't the only parent to do this) until the bell went and we all went in. It was easy to see her there from the playground because the fence and gate were of the chain link type, so I would stand watching her with the fearful, lonely day before me, while she anxiously observed me from the road, if I went to the toilet (they were at the far end of the playground in this old school) which I very often did worried in case I was caught out in class, I would rush back in order to see Mother one more time before the bell went. Once the bell had gone it all got a lot worse, for at the instigation of a teacher's whistle all the children had to form up in their individual classes by lining up in pairs. Of course, having nobody to pair up with meant I was pushed to the end of the line, each and every morning. Apparently on one occasion I ran out of the school to rejoin Mother as the bell rang... my mother's quick solution for this was to ask another passing child... an older girl to take me back and hold my hand in the line, I don't know if she did this or not, because as I have explained I can't remember any of this. But this I do know, the very writing of this event has caused a powerful emotional reaction. It started with a spontaneous feeling of panic together with an impulse to run... run anywhere as if in a terrible turmoil, linked to this urge was a fear of running; then within minutes the crying started welling up from deep within me, the adult now had just become a spectator, my raw child was back evoked by these few written words concerning Greenhill School. Just sometimes along with such unbidden emotions insight may follow, a sudden connection made between the past and a present symptom and today just now, this has occurred. For years now one of my intrusive thoughts has been as described above, 'the sudden panic feeling and impulse to run' and now I believe I know where this intrusion originates. Under the extreme stress of the playground situation, panicking and yet still fearful of the consequences I ran to Mother for protection, the slightly older child had yielded to the terrified infant within. That's why I experienced the panic/ run intrusion when I considered writing about this incident... the old fear and anguish was evoked and revealed at a conscious level as the strange feeling of panic. While the impulse to run that was associated with the original fear situation, now intruded upon my consciousness in the form of intrusive urge to once again do the same.

The 2011 example is more even obviously traumatic in nature and relates I'm sure to a much earlier event in my life, although this time within the spontaneous text there is no direct reference to any particular situation.

7th February 2011

While passing the [my] house *[driving past on the way to a supermarket]* I suddenly become aware of my raw child, wanting to go home. This grew in emotional power and next I wanted to cry, [my raw child] seemed to be saying, 'I want to go home mummy!' This [subject] seems to be the start of this episode... I had to stop at a lay-by the crying was so powerful. Returning home my raw child was very close and upset... once home I gave way to the emotion [and] a great deal of crying followed [linked to] a sort of sobbing and whimpering. Along with this was the following [spontaneous] communication:

Mummy help, me.

Go home, mummy... want to go home.

[A feeling of] despair!

Mummy, mummy! [shouting this]

Very frightened... very, very frightened.

[The powerful crying and sobbing continue throughout]

Despair... despair, giving up!

Utter despair [mumbled] mummy, mummy, mummy [followed] by wordless whimpering... utter, utter despair.

[More] whimpering just whimpering. Can't think anymore/ anything.

Just whimpering and more whimpering, mummy, mummy... oh mummy, oh mummy!

[Note written at the time] my raw child, this part of me knows <u>absolute</u> despair.

At the end of chapter one I mentioned the short period in hospital I underwent aged two and quarter for a circumcision. I am convinced that the above intrusive communication; is the child's memory of that event, still emotionally active within my raw child complex. These few fleeting thoughts captured as a written record obviously recall an experience that was truly traumatic in nature; even so the words fail to convey the sheer strength of the emotional accompaniment. This was overwhelmingly powerful, the crying had a physical component, which shook my whole body and it was difficult to breathe through the sobbing. Along with the crying came feelings of intense fear, utter despair and outright panic, none of which I felt at the time I could ever escape. As stated before (in chapter one) although this episode was very traumatic I don't believe it was the origin of my fundamental anxiety, nor the cause of the dissociation (separating up) of my inner self, into the three distinct aspects this book has given prominence to throughout. Rather the early hospital experience helped fix the way my inner fears and doubts were formulated and later portrayed in symptoms. It played its part by giving rise to some of the sensitivities and propensities within my dissociated child complexes, helping to form the fearful, conforming child, laden down with his fears of illness, punishment and hospital, and by way of a reaction the opposite angry resentful child... who rebels and hits out. It was just one facet (though perhaps an important one) of a host of other life experiences that together were to make the content of my OCD unique to me. What then was the fundamental cause of this complex symptomatology that was worthy of the label OCD? Well I believe that I became predisposed to developing this curious disorder, chiefly because of the presence within my psyche of these dissociated infantile complexes. Once formed these became both the cause and the source of the disorder, for their presence made me particularly sensitive and vulnerable to certain life events, while their continued activity and interaction with each other and with the adult me, produced the intrusions upon my awareness that constitute my symptoms. In my case the dissociation that give rise to these complexes, had its origins in my general anxiousness as a child and specifically in my overprotected and exclusive relationship with my mother… much more on this in the last chapter.

The last two examples are extreme illustrations of the effect upon the adult me when my raw child complex was particularly active or close. But these exceptionally strong intrusions are rare and usually only occurred within the already high emotional state of a 'return' like those described earlier in the chapter. Most instances of the child's influence are much more subtle in nature, consisting of sudden emotions or irrational ideas that are at once noticed because they are so at odds with my normal thinking and I have already given a number of examples of this happening. Sometimes my raw child's influence would persist in certain circumstances to constantly disrupt and undermine my thinking for days at a time. A good example of this occurred in 1984 when my wife and I went on holiday to Devon with my parents. As had happened before in other such holidays, living with my parents even for a week seemed to evoke the old dependant relationship within me and along with the feelings of vulnerability and fear this awakened, there inevitably appeared the angry opposite reaction in the form of intrusive thoughts of violence.

Saturday 11th August 1984
While travelling [to Devon] got sudden feeling of anxiety and fear and I felt as if people were looking at me [an old symptom].
[Reflective note made at the time] dismissed these feelings as being fear of being away from home.
Arrived [at holiday home] more sudden feelings of fear… fear of something unknown.

Sunday
The anxiety feelings are worse, fear and panic at being ill or becoming ill. All fears became worse when I had to sit down and eat *[another common trigger in me]*. *[Reflective note made at the time]* these fears seem to be about, if I felt ill now *[because of the anxiety, which is very good at stopping one eating]* I would not be able to eat and so become more ill… this [idea] makes me panic.
But it was also as if I wanted to panic or frighten myself with these ideas, to stop myself eating.

147

[Feeling like this] anything, any thought can make me panic. I've become afraid of the dark, and of becoming alone in same strange way, but strongest of all is this fear of becoming ill.

That night I had a significant dream about my 'run back home' at the age of 15. It is not show here because it appears with interpretation in the chapter dedicate to dreams.

Monday

Today I feel much better, the panic and the anxiety feelings seem to have left me. *[Reflective note made at the time]* this change in feelings must be due I believe to the outcome of [last night's] dream, it must have reduced my feelings of anxiety and anger *[I was having numerous violent intrusive thoughts]*. All these feelings I have suffered over the past few days were just indications of an unconscious drama being acted out [within me] the dream just showed this more clearly. Nothing I could do during the day had any effect on this unconscious problem, the dream had to provide the answer, until then I was just a victim of what was going on unconsciously.

Tuesday

On Tuesday I was all right until I bought a book about ghosts [ghosts of Devon or some such book] later that day as soon as I started reading this book, I became very frightened. I felt very alone as if no one could help me, [then] I seemed to remember being a little child again about 4 perhaps and remembered how I was frightened of things, unknown things... the anxiety feelings have retuned.

Thursday

[Today] I suddenly feel as if my parents are somehow against me, as if they have changed towards me. This all reminds me of when I left school at 15. This feeling makes me feel even jealous of my wife when I felt she had more food on her plate than me.

[Reflective note made at the time] I have the idea that my [intrusive] fear of people changing is to do with how I felt my parents changed towards me when I left school.

[Later]

when visiting churches, I get an increased number of intrusive thoughts, [these include] the usual violent ones and the impulse to think and shout out at God... even though I fear these ideas and [the possibility] that I might actually shout something.

[Reflective note made at the time] I see this anger at God just like the anger at my parents, [I feel it's linked to] when at 15 I thought both had let me down.

[Also today] I had a general fear of being out in the world... I felt unsafe, a fear of things changing. All this reminds me of when I was 15, fears of things changing is also the fear of growing older.

From the above details it can be appreciated that throughout most of this holiday week, my everyday 'normal' thinking and hence my relationship with others and my enjoyment of the holiday etc., was disturbed by numerous intrusive thoughts and invasive emotions. As stated the very act of living with my parents seems to have triggered my raw child complex and along with him as was so often the norm my angry rebel aspect quickly appears also. With both complexes active the adult me was once again beset with symptoms reflecting their different natures. The irrational fears of the raw child as seen in the ghost book event, counterbalanced by my angry child's rage represented in the constant intrusive impulses. To this mix of unbidden thoughts and emotions must of course be added the anxiety evoked at a conscious level in response to these intrusions, and I believe it possible that some of the initial anxiety (on Saturday) was due to an inner perception that the rational adult me was under threat from within. This example is unusual because the actual understanding of the connection between the triggering situation and the symptoms didn't come from a reasoned consideration at the time or from later insight, but from a dream, the dream of Sunday night. This by its content, it was all about the difficult period I spent at home when I ran away from my first job, (see chapter two) connected this short period of living back with my parents to the symptoms this evoked… by showing me what emotionally charged memories had been unconsciously activated.

The next example which is the very last I shall give in this chapter describes a chance experience that caused a powerful awakening of my raw child complex, I say awakening here because prior to this incident I had been relatively free of any kind of intrusion for some time. This fact led me to believe that these other aspects of myself although sometimes undetectable at a conscious level, and thus producing the feeling of awakening when they do suddenly appear, are nevertheless constantly aware and functioning in parallel to my ordinary adult thinking... how else could a sudden triggering event be it internal or external elicit such a rapid response. Also because the trigger here was a single clear-cut event the resultant dual response to it is equally as transparent. On the surface this event appears totally unrelated to me personally and yet it managed to produce an intrusive response so completely different to my adult reaction, that there was obviously considerable unconscious sensitivity present of which I was initially entirely ignorant. Occurring in the year 2000 during a holiday to Cornwall this incident has always been a powerful reminder to me of my inner duality, well in my case a triplicity really if one counts the two child complexes and the adult me... in fact I've frequently joked that in certain situations, 'I'm in three minds'... although of course the reality of this, bearing in mind the effect upon my life... has alas been no joke.

21st July 2000

On Friday evening went for a last walk to cape Cornwall *[we were leaving to return home the following day]*. Here by the sea in an ordinary field so it seemed was a lone grave of an 8-year-old child, I think it was a boy [from the symbolism it appeared Buddhist]. Over the grave had been placed a number of toys, I remember a car and one of those 'electronic play mates' so popular at the time. For some reason I initially thought the date on the gravestone was 1947, my father and son later corrected this when they told me the date was really 1997 this meant for me that the toys were actually his, not just left years later. While first seeing the grave 'I' had just acknowledged its poignancy intellectually, there had been no personal connection or emotion. Later after returning to our holiday home my son mentioned again the child's grave with all their toys on top… at once I became aware of my raw child who was crying and completely broken-hearted about the little child alone on that dark hill side. With his toys, which he had once played with and loved… the toys he could no longer even touch, my raw child was most particularly upset about the little electronic game, who he imagined the little boy loving the most and now it was just lying in the wet and cold… no longer working. My child complex was filled with intense grief and sorrow [as he] thought again and again of the placing of the toys on the grave on that day in 1997.

[Reflective note made at the time] the above is a very good example of the duality possible in the mind. When I the adult me looked at that grave my raw child complex

also perceived it and reacted independently of me in a way determined by the nature of the complex. I unaware of this, felt only the everyday response of the adult me, and this [I believed] denied my raw child's opportunity to give expression to his feelings at the grave. *[In other words the dissociation within me prevented my acknowledgement and appreciation of my full emotional repertoire… I had to wait until the other emotions attached to my child complex appeared intrusively, before I could fully realise how 'I' truly felt].*

[Later]
My raw child is very still active, he 'told' me what he wanted to do (in an image form) he wanted to leave a little toy himself on the grave. *[This need was quite compulsive and thus difficult to resist, but time and distance restraints did in fact prevent me from ever going back.]*

In summary, the main purpose of this chapter has been to attempt to convince the reader, as indeed I have come to be convinced that within my psyche there is a still active infantile aspect, which has persisted fundamentally unchanged from my earliest childhood. The precise nature of this aspect I did not define, and I believe it almost impossible to do so, rather I have instead described how this complex appears to the observing adult me… and that is, as a mini autonomous personality with its own emotional identity, memories and cognitive ability. Although beyond my rational control or even scrutiny this dissociated complex retains the ability to thrust its ideology into my awareness, the capacity to do this being the origin of some at least of my intrusive thoughts and invasive emotions. Over the years I have many times experienced the inner influence of this child complex and especially during the periods I have come to call 'returns' when he appeared very close or active, periods that corresponded with heightened anxiety and intensified OCD type symptoms. Although symptoms would change as they interacted with my adult self and my ever-changing life situation in general, I noticed the essential essence of this child; his nature if you like remained consistently the same. This could be observed in what he reacted to and in the manner this reaction took, as well as in the overall way he presented himself within my personality. An explicit example of the latter is the sudden unbidden 'shouting' of mummy, mummy along with a feeling of undefined fear, this common intrusion into my awareness indicating I'm sure that this aspect of myself had been provoked and is responding accordingly. When experiencing such obviously childlike intrusions it is difficult, I'm sure the reader will agree to personally rebut the notion of the continuance of the child within the adult.

Central to the character of this child complex is the thinking and fears that dominated my actual childhood years; he is a timid, anxious and mother fixed little boy and so was I the child that grew under that inner influence. Even my earliest recollections of myself reveal this timid and fearful nature, this acknowledgement strengthens my belief that the fearful child aspect was formed very early on in my childhood and although I (as an older child) was not aware of the extreme hurt and terror locked away within this complex, it did govern and distort my subsequent development. Hence I remained attached to home inherently fearful of the world beyond its confines... afraid of other people and timid in their presence I became a pleaser to keep in with them at any cost and my resultant total lack of self-assertion prevented any show of individuality and hindered my maturation. Add to this the specific child fears revolving around hospital and illness, and illness as a punishment linked to excessive guilt, and we have an individual unable to deal with the demands of the growing up... which were nevertheless abruptly forced upon me when I left school. That's why I suffered a breakdown at that point in my life among the emotional turmoil of that period was a need to run back to home and Mother for protection. During that time the young child within the adolescent largely hidden until then, returned; much to the bewilderment and anguish of the young adult me, and when my inner needs failed to be met and I found myself pushed back out into the world... a world I still couldn't deal with, yet another previously hidden and forgotten aspect of my psyche was to appear. This one had a nature that greatly shocked and scared me, nevertheless as I was to learn many years later, it was a part of me my raw child knew well and thus must have been present from my earliest years. This newly released rebel personality so full of anger and negativism, so contrary, so opposite in every way to the conforming adult and the fearful timid child me, seemed able to threaten both of us. A new kid was on the block and a new episode in my OCD... and life had just begun.

Chapter Six

The Rebel within

Even when my raw child complex was active and experienced directly, it was in a way no more than an extreme version of the fears and doubts I had known throughout my childhood and indeed still knew as an adult. But the tendency this chapter deals with later known as Rebel, seemed to have no such personal history, inasmuch as I didn't recognize its oppositional, angry and repugnant thoughts as any characteristic or feature belonging to myself. These intrusions just seemed to come out of nowhere and once present they threatened the very integrity of my nature; in a way my raw child never could. The reason for this unfamiliarity with rebel's nature occurred I believe because this complex remained completely concealed from my conscious awareness during my early years, something my raw child aspect was never to do. For although I never touched the child's raw emotional power directly, until my breakdown at the age of 15, I was nevertheless as stated before highly influenced by it and over time came to identify with its tendencies. As this did not occur with the rebel complex its nature so opposing and different, profoundly shocked and disturbed the timid, self-effacing and conforming conscious me. Even though I didn't recognize these thoughts… they were still my thoughts, within my head… this fact I naturally acknowledged however alien the thoughts were to my known personality. But if I didn't recognize them how did I begin to understand their presence and origin in me? Well as the earlier chapters have described the meanings behind the thoughts usually violent intrusions in the case of Rebel, became gradually clear after years of observing when and where they appeared. But the insight into the origins of Rebel came from a different source in fact by way of spontaneous (intrusive) information during the times my raw child was particularly active or close, such as during the 'returns' I have described earlier. Those insights provide evidence my Rebel complex was not born out of the emotional turmoil that followed my leaving school, but rather he was resurrected during that period. For although I didn't recognize him he had nevertheless been part of my early child personality. It is to Rebel's origins that I first turn to in this chapter dedicated to him, as usual all information comes from my psychological diaries or therapy notes.

19th June 1993

While looking at a photograph of me as a small child, something I very much wanted to keep safe, I had a sudden intrusive thought/ image to tear it up. This was immediately followed by a [very early] memory of 'breaking things I really want' while angry or in a rage. This is the first time I've remembered this and without doubt it was linked to the intrusive thought.

23rd August 1993

I was thinking… worrying about my important letters *[all the paperwork I very much wanted to keep]* when suddenly a Rebel [intrusive] thought/ image to tear them all up appeared.

While shopping I sometimes yielded (especially after I understood the nature of my raw child complex) to feelings bubbling up from within, concerning a toy 'we' had seen. The following two examples illustrate what occurred when I bought a small model car for my raw child aspect.

7th February 1994

Today when I offered the little car I had bought for my raw child *[deliberate imagined interaction with this other part of me].* there were two immediate spontaneous reactions, firstly, happy to take it and wanting it very much. Secondly, throwing it down at once in anger. How many times has this dual reaction occurred within my life…raw child and then Rebel. [Are they] parts of the same child? How much this throwing down of the car reminds me of the [memory] 'breaking things I really want' and of the mother going away dream *[this dream is discussed in the next chapter]*.

9th February 2011

[While at the supermarket I] bought a little car for my raw child… tears came to 'his' eyes straight away. [But a little] later back at home something had changed; there was now an impulse to throw the car down in anger. 'Breaking things I want' was back … [another example of] Rebel had appeared.

When I recorded the above I had quite naturally forgotten all about the earlier similar event, and without my psychological diaries the connection between the two, which indicates a consistency of response across the years, would have probably remained unidentified.

This example alone thus demonstrates the importance of keeping a journal… for recurring themes, which are the fundamental building blocks to self- understanding are very readily picked up on by this simple method. Of course these two examples show a direct intrusion into my awareness of an impulse to throw down the object in my hand after a certain precipitating event. But I have also often experienced this angry intrusion without any pervious triggering activity or indeed with anything in my hand, it seemed in general that this impulse was a general indicator of an inner rage, which at a conscious level I knew nothing about. In addition, the same tendency could influence the rational adult me in more subtle ways and often did, as the next diary record shows.

30th December 2006

Went shopping with my wife and picked out a jacket for myself, after deciding I would definitely have it I had this feeling to put it back… deny myself it. At the same time, it was all a bit of a show, I wanted my wife to know how I felt… to almost demonstrate to her the action of rejecting the jacket. The underlying feeling seemed to be once again 'breaking what I really want' and in this example I wanted the jacket but at the same time it was necessary to show this to my wife I didn't… anger was also present. It seemed as if I was [refusing] an offer from my wife, despite the fact that it was all my doing.

[Reflective note made at the time] it seems here that my wife is Mother. Mother offers (something) that my raw child wants very much, but [then] Rebel's anger pushes it away.

The feeling of needing to deny myself something I actually want expressed in ways very similar to the above, together with the attention demanding behaviour it provokes, is very common occurrence in me and I could give many examples of its appearance. They all represent I believe at an adult level the same underlying angry rejection that appears in a more authentic form, as the

161

intrusive impulses. The following provide a little more insight into this curious duality.

23rd August 1993

[Suddenly] I have a memory/ feeling of breaking things up in anger, while feeling sad/ crying for losing them.

23rd December 1993

This memory/ idea of 'breaking what I really want' goes back a long way. I seem to be able to remember my mother saying something about this attitude in me, when I was angry as a child.

28th December 1993

Also *[related to the diary entry above]* there is a strong need to draw attention to the act of 'breaking what I really want'.

It is important to note here that sudden memories such as those above were not an everyday event; they tended to appear during periods of heightened symptoms and increased anxiety, in other words when the complexes responsible for the symptoms were particularly active or close. I have discovered that during such times the complexes could sometimes give themselves away as it were, and material underlying the symptom could occasionally appear with it, if this did occur there was a chance for additional understanding of the symptom itself. The best illustration of this being the very first example in this chapter (dated the 19th June 93) where the symptom, the intrusion impulse to tear up a photo of me, was followed by a childhood memory of 'breaking things I really want'. This provided me with the insight that the angry impulse emanated from an infantile anger with a tendency to act in a certain way. It would seem then that Rebel's tendencies in the past were witnessed by my raw child; in fact, of course they knew each other well, as they were both aspects of my early childhood personality. So how did this timid and anxious part of me regard the angry and oppositional part, well the following diary entries show the relationship clearly.

12th August 1982
Old memories: I am aware of a small child crying bitterly as I want to cry for him, frightened of being bad in mummy's eyes.

14th December 1992
[Part of a larger note] the anxiety caused by the very strong Rebel impulses seemed to evoke my raw child and produce the [spontaneous] thought, 'Mother save me!'

10th May 1995
When I had a Rebel thought I suddenly became aware of my raw child 'saying' *[spontaneous intrusion]* 'I don't want to be bad' and a real feeling of fear associated with this. Is this an indication of the old problem [is] my raw child frightened of Rebel?

[Reflective note made at the time] when close to my raw child like this I get the feeling that he is afraid of Rebel and had 'pushed' away Rebel (the angry little boy) because he was scared of losing Mother's love. At 15 both 'children' appeared again [first the frightened child] and then when I was rejected by Mother (i.e. lost her love) there was then nothing to keep Rebel in check and he appeared also.

5th June 1995

At lunchtime got Rebel thoughts and [the next instant] my raw child was crying for mummy, the two appearances seemed to be linked. It is as if my raw child was frightened/ felt out of control of the Rebel part of 'himself' and was crying for mother's help. Was this how it was when I was very young?

12th June 1995

[My] symptoms start suddenly, fears of being bad… quickly followed by a feeling/ memory of saying, 'I'm not bad mummy… I'm not bad mummy!'

[Reflective note made at the time] my raw child has a powerful feeling of being bad; when this expresses itself [via] me *[i.e. when I experience it 'bubbling up from within']* it's an absolute fear, like the end of the world.

[Additional note made at the time] these feelings of being bad (raw child feelings) gives rise to a lot of [other] symptoms. For example, the following:

a) The guilt dreams [in which I have done something bad and expect/ fear punishment].

b) The guilt feelings [intrusive 'convictions' I have done something bad, when obviously this is not the case].

c) Sudden [intrusive] fears of being a bad person or of me becoming bad [this includes the irrational fear of contamination i.e. reading or hearing about a bad person could make me the same as them].

d) Fears of being punished [a continuation of the fears of childhood].

e) Fears that I wouldn't know right from wrong [a sort of philosophical doubt about myself, but based I believe on this early feeling of being bad, a feeling which I just cannot eradicate].

But whatever the final associated symptom, the original fear of being bad seems [fundamentally] linked to mummy leaving and a fear of losing mummy by being bad.

4th April 1995

My raw child told me today *[intrusive emotionally charged idea]* that he is afraid of losing mummy by being bad, like a bad person, a wicked person because then he would be all alone.

[Note made next day]

my raw child has been very close to me this week… this has reminded me of how bad he feels. His fears were about people dying, being alone and being a bad person, and such fears they are... I must not underestimate them [for they have the potential to overwhelm my adult rational mind].

12th June 1997
My raw child has been very active over the [past] few weeks and as usual because of this, the anger/ rage of Rebel has also returned. Raw child feels very afraid and guilty about some of Rebel's opposite thoughts and seems to be crying and saying, 'I'm not bad... I'm not bad!' This seems to remind me of my early childhood... of wanting to be good [but apparently] being aware and frightened of the angry and resenting little boy within me. I (the adult me) must remember that Rebel always does and thinks the very opposite from the raw child

From the above selection I hope the reader can appreciate the nature of the relationship between these two child aspects within me. I believe the intrusive material self-evidently reveals that my raw child was terrified of being a bad boy; because to be so would he believed result in the loss of Mother's love and protection. In me this feared bad aspect is personified in the form of Rebel, the angry, negative and oppositional child... the very antithesis of his timid, fearful and conforming sibling. This fear of being bad is further illustrated albeit in a different form in the following two sudden memories.

2nd October 1993

Early morning: sudden ideas about doubting my mother's love for me (the raw child me) after I had been bad.

10th September 1993

[This] lunchtime a lot of emotion appeared (crying) I had felt this as tension within me beforehand. I suddenly remembered how at the beginning of this period [when this 'return' had begun] my raw child appeared bad. Later when thinking about this a sudden memory surfaced, of me following my mother around to see if she still loved me... after doing something to hurt her [feelings].

[Further notes made at the time] the [intrusive] thoughts have returned of only having a little thing and nothing else, a great amount of emotion (crying) was linked to this.

Also everyday things [rubbish] being thrown away caused an emotional response, [I was] sad to see them go, as if they were alive.

This last diary entry also strongly reveals the multifaceted nature of these complexes for although the initial intrusion was a sudden recollection of an incident with my mother; it was very quickly followed by other more general feelings and altered thinking of a type that indicated my raw child was close. This tendency for diverse interaction is not at all unusual, for a complex has a repertoire of possible disruptions depending on its disposition and complexity and thus can have a broad range of effects upon the individual's consciousness. Indeed, the sudden memory itself was a 'product' of this complex's activity ... in other words this was a memory retained by the child, but unknown to the adult me until that sudden recollection that day. Although all this had occurred at lunchtime I had been aware of this increased activity in the form of tension within me since the early morning, and the spontaneous crying merely confirmed for me the presence of my raw child. This diary entry then like most of the others in this chapter is all raw child and any reference to Rebel or of the badness associated with him, is from that child's point of view. I find I cannot write much at all directly from Rebel's perspective for as stated in the introduction to this chapter, I do not know him directly. All I have is the rebel of my past as perceived by his mother fixed and timid sibling, and my adult experience of rebel's anger and opposite thinking as contained within the intrusive thoughts. But despite those limitations I now believe my raw child's emotionally changed memories of his angry opposite are particularly telling and accurate, because even though they appear as separate identities now within my psyche, they were I'm sure originally parts of the same child, but more of this in the final chapter for now the next group of examples show how closely bound together these two are.

24th April 1995

[My raw child is] close to me today, he is fearful about being bad. I try to reassure him, but all I get is that he does indeed feel he is a bad boy... something Mother told him [I wonder].

[Later]
as above, talking to my raw child trying to reassure him that he isn't bad... suddenly what I said seemed to lose effect. A [strong] feeling of fear, fear of being bad was blocking what I said. My raw child seemed to fear something... a bad part was there, something else was there! This had the effect of frightening even [the adult] me.

[Later]
while thinking who else could be there [what other aspect of me that is] after the above event...I suddenly had Rebel like symptoms... was it just Rebel 'down there'? Later while thinking about all this again I get the feeling that Rebel although rejected because of his tantrums, still wanted to be held, loved and protected. Is he (Rebel) what my raw child is afraid of... did Rebel split off from him years ago?

22nd March 2004
Tonight Rebel and then my raw child are very close, the same old way of expressing themselves (my symptoms) Rebel's anger appears first and then raw child's fears. Why always in that order except in 1972 (first outbreak) when raw child appears first (well the derivatives of him i.e. the symptoms) then the anger of rebel follows as I am

rejected. The more overt signs of raw child then disappear, but Rebel remains producing most of my symptoms until 1982. [That year] during that bad period at the start of treatment [when] I discovered my raw child again. Then he shrinks back once more leaving Rebel producing symptoms at a lower intensity. In 1993 reading up my old notes evoked another return of raw child and again he appeared in 1995 *[caused by the chance seeing of the gravestone with 'Daddy and Mum' on].*

[Reflective note made at the time] my raw child's personality is well represented in the adult me, i.e. I express his needs (feel guilty and try to please others etc.). But Rebel not so much therefore he appears much more in intrusive ideas.

1st April 1994

Raw child still active today I wonder if this little 'return' started [as usual] with the upsurge of violent thoughts that occurred earlier, and then [things] moved on quickly to the fears of my raw child.

3rd May 1995

With my little raw child at lunchtime trying to reassure him he isn't bad, when suddenly the block appears again, [that is] the feeling of being bad had appeared. As if there is something 'bad down there' with my raw child. What! … What could it be? A fear of badness, a conviction of being bad… an event, a memory, taken as proof that I'm bad. Whatever it is, it is responsible for this powerful emotional belief belonging to my raw child personality and for a host of related symptoms.

[Note made at the time] Earlier the same day the feeling of unknowing fear (of the type linked to my raw child) came over me. It reminded me of being at school aged 10 fearing illness and feeling I would be safe at home with Mother.

[Later that day]

later it seems that my fearful thoughts are linked to stories, film and things seen on T.V. *[All common examples of raw child's fears].*

18th December 2010

More insight? Remember my raw child is very close to me at the moment, therefore I feel how he feels now and [thus] in the past. Today I still have this feeling of something else... frightening, threatening the child and me. [While considering this] I suddenly became aware of my raw child saying (to Mother); he was frightened of being bad, as if scared of something within him. My raw child is scared of his own anger just as if it was an outside influence... hence this strange feeling now [something fearful and threatening within] and the irrational fear of being contaminated by bad people or evil in general.

Of course it must be remembered that my first fear of contamination by badness relates to my mother's warning not to have the same mad eyes of father or grandfather (the so called Collins look) when they were in a rage (see chapter one).

[Returning to the 18th December later on that day]
I (the adult me) just had the horrible experience of feeling I couldn't trust anything/ anyone in the whole world… this was followed this time [I've had these feelings before] by a spontaneous [intrusive] image of my little raw child overwhelmed by such feelings in a certain situation… was this situation the hospital visit when I was two? He (my raw child) felt he couldn't trust anyone anymore… anyone could turn horrible!

[Later still]
this note is about Rebel; while writing out the above I suddenly felt a feeling of relief and understanding I was reassured that I understood my symptoms from the context of my raw child's fears etc. Immediately there followed a Rebel intrusive thought in the form of an image, of me angrily chasing my raw child in order to hurt him. This is a typical Rebel opposite and conflicting response, I'm feeling ok and at one with my raw child so an intrusion appears to disrupt and spoil things.

I imagine the reader at this point will want an explanation of what I have just described, and yes as strange as it seems this is an example of a hostile intrusive thought being directed at an aspect of my own internal mental world. In all other ways similar to those intrusions triggered by and directed at the external world, these internally directed equivalents were not that uncommon. I hope this curious tendency helps illustrate to the reader the idea of a conflict within the individual... when one is at odds with oneself, for certainly that is the way I experience OCD.

23rd January 2011

This morning while still in bed, felt vulnerable [my little raw child was very close to me] and after some intrusive ideas, I had an image of me saying to my wife (in a panic) I've got frightening thoughts! This was followed by a [seemingly intrusive] memory of me telling my mother this, was my raw child [so] bothered by these thoughts... I already know he was so afraid of being bad.

Now this diary entry really shows the complex interrelationship between past and present and between the different 'players' within my psyche, in psychological jargon the very psychodynamics of me. Initially on this day I become aware of my timid and anxious child aspect via the feeling of vulnerability that 'percolated up' from within. Then following a series of rebel type thoughts that frightened this 'child' so much that he sought reassurance from my wife, just as he had from my mother in the past, an event confirmed by the sudden memory. Both events perhaps separated by at least 50 years were appeals for help to a significant person, Mother in my early childhood but my wife now, who is plainly seen as mother to my raw child complex. No better example of the past informing the present could I feel be asked for... for this one episode of intrusions, demonstrates not only the old relationship between Rebel and the raw child, and their ability to affect the adult me now, but also clearly shows how my relationship with significant individuals now are influenced by those of the past. The next two diary notes further illustrate these internal dynamics.

24th March 2004

This morning my wife appears to look at me in an exasperated way [a continuation of the problems we're having at the moment] at once there is an aggressive [Rebel] impulse... very frightening, which causes me (the adult me) a pang of anxiety. Suddenly it comes to me that my little raw child is afraid of this anger [part of the anxious response had been his] because of its consequences i.e. Mother (my wife in this case) would leave me, not love me anymore and so I would be all alone. Although I call this angry child Rebel... he is of course part of my raw child [personality]. Therefore [effectively] my raw child is terrified of his own anger... that's why there is a Rebel.

22nd November 2000

Smiley tooth *[an important homemade toy]* was on the mantelpiece when I considered lighting the fire. Immediately I had an [intrusive] image/ feeling of Smiley tooth being in the fire... being 'killed' [my raw child believes Smiley tooth is indeed alive] and a feeling of loss. I [experienced] both an impulse to throw Smiley tooth into the fire and the sadness of losing him. Here we have my little raw child who loves Smiley tooth and fears losing him, while Rebel (who always does the opposite) prompts 'us' into throwing him into the fire. I get the feeling that this duality is from my very earliest years, my raw child and Rebel have often felt [this way] and fought before.

Once again in the above we see the familiar raw child and Rebel relationship together as usual, but apparently separate aspects within my psyche. But I end this chapter with a final group of recorded encounters where a blurring of this distinction may be seen. This insight occurred mainly when my child complexes were very active or close, which remember corresponded with the adult me being particularly ill. Sometimes during such periods Rebel's anger would alternate rapidly with the raw child's fear, in other words I experienced intrusive feelings of intense anger followed by equally painfully strong feeling of fear, before this in turn was displaced by the anger again and so on... and just sometimes when in such turmoil it would appear that it was the raw child himself who was in a rage, quite independently of Rebel. Were Rebel and my raw child somehow combined during these periods, time to look at the actual recorded experiences?

21st September 1982

Childish things keep coming up, fear of being alone, of being left alone. Then feelings of hatred and anger... I seem to alternate between these two feelings.

30th June 1995

Today around lunchtime I was feeling very frustrated because of my symptoms and the feeling I just didn't know what to do to help my little raw child. There was quite a lot of crying, but not much insight as to why... it seemed to be mixed with anger. Later this happened again [i.e. the crying and anger together] perhaps this is a good thing.

22nd March 2011

[While writing about the time I ran back home at the age of 15 (see chapter two) the following spontaneously occurred]. While I write this the emotion I feel is raw [I mean] raw now in 2011 [even though the event was 39 years ago]. There is crying and anger one after the other... as if my raw child and Rebel are together. Next the emotional acknowledgement came to me that 'I needed to be a little boy again, protected/ loved etc. and all I got was shit! [This statement being linked to my view I had been rejected and pushed back out to work before I was ready]. Then the anger and crying started again, over and over again.

[Later my thoughts return again to when I was 15, this time I remember the terrible arguments with my mother... once more the emotions are strong and close].

When thinking about the shouting, 'I hate you' (at my mother) I actually try it and at once broke down crying with my little raw child 'shouting' mummy, mummy. When I try it again there is a feeling of loving Mother at the same time [as I'm shouting I hate her] there is alternating love and hate here in the same child... being directed at the same person.

15th December 2012
While reading about when I was 15 (the 22-3-2011 note) the emotion evoked was raw and there was (intrusive) anger and crying... one after the other. Now this is happening once more, my raw child has been close for over a month since the visit to the vets, [with our cat Tinker] but he was close anyway because of this writing about me [this book]. Now of course Rebel is present and active as well. So I am [experiencing] the following, intense thoughts of anger and violence together with crying, fear and panic. It is if I'm close to, or reliving an emotionally charged event, similar to what the important dream alludes to *[this dream is discussed in the next chapter]*. I feel a mix of crying for/ needing and hating this same person... who must be Mother.

[Reflective note made at the time] these feelings then get displaced on to others, [my wife for example] when I'm in the grip of this intrusive anger and fear of it... it feels like [being in the middle] of a small child's tantrum. The fear of and the intensity of the anger is much worse when I'm

in this raw child state, as if I'm close to the emotional origin.

17th December 2012

[This afternoon] great emotion from my little raw child about Tinker, he is crying bitterly and is 'shouting' I don't want her to die... I don't want her to die. The emotion (the crying) returns as I write this note, I think this emotion within me is causing the panic feelings that in turn remind me of when I was 15. Perhaps this feeling of anger (the emotion only) has a similar origin... it feels as if my raw child aspect can't deal with his feelings.

18th December 2012

During this return not only has there been intense emotion with my raw child crying often and sometimes bitterly. There has also been a feeling of turmoil and panic that spontaneously reminds me of when I was 15. But now there seems to be anger (just the emotion) ready to attach itself to any event or person. Because my raw child is so close at the moment, am I experiencing how I felt when I ran back home from my first job? There was emotional turmoil then, crying and anger combined... and all mainly related to my mother.

21st January 2013

I'm determined to get to the bottom of this outbreak of symptoms. There is no doubt in my mind that this particular activation [this return] of my raw child and

Rebel is due to Tinkers illness. This trigger/ stressor has evoked in my raw child a turmoil of very powerful emotions... feelings he just cannot accept [namely] Tinker may die. Consequently, there are panic feelings, a feeling of being out of control, despair, distress, anger and much crying, all mixed together. There is something about this type of panic that reminds me of when I was 15, and the adult me now seems 'used up' as it were... and thus I find it difficult to function day to day, any additional problems however slight are too much for me.

[Earlier note written on the 20th December 2013 used here on the 21st to support the above statements].
Today I started getting feelings/ ideas of being out of control also of panic and frustration. Often now there is an intrusive image/ impulse of throwing something down in a fit of anger, a feeling of not knowing what to do is mixed with anger and crying. I feel as if I'm in the middle of a childish tantrum, some of this feels/ reminds me of when I was 15. So it seems this trigger event (Tinker's illness) is as powerful as leaving school was in evoking my little raw child complex, this must be so because the nature and level of the panic reminds me so much of how I felt at 15. The emotional intensity of this 'return' is an indication of just how upset my raw child aspect has become, he just can't and won't accept Tinker is dying, he can't deal with the feelings this evokes, it's like an emotional overload to him that's why there are all these strange feelings of [inner] turmoil... of distress, despair and anger all at once.

My little raw child is in the midst of a tantrum that's why he feels out of control. But the unexpected thing here is the anger associated with all this seems to belong to my raw child himself… it is <u>not</u> separate in, nor expressed via Rebel, but of course I always knew he and Rebel were but different aspects of the same child complex.

In summary, although the aspect of me personified as Rebel has appeared throughout this story as the challenging and angry origin of my intrusive opposing and violent thoughts, this chapter looked to establish his origin and Rebel's nature within my personal history. Despite appearing to first emerge from the turmoil at home that followed my first job, Rebel, I have tried to show was not a creation of that period but rather those circumstances caused him to be resurrected as it were, from my past. For early memories some of which spontaneously appeared along with intrusive thoughts, reveal that rebel was present from my early childhood and was often linked to my raw child aspect, who greatly feared him… as Rebel's perverse character threatened that child's relationship with Mother. In fact, it would seem likely that my raw child's idea that he is a bad boy and the associated guilt generated by this, is due to the presence of Rebel, and the many examples of the spontaneous sensing of something bad within me… behind or with my raw child aspect, has I believe the same explanation. Indeed, on at least one occasion (the 24th April 1995 diary entry) Rebel type intrusions accompanied these powerful feelings of something bad within. Even though my raw child and Rebel complexes for the most part manifested themselves within my psyche as separate entities, the final part of this chapter dealt with the apparent blurring of this distinction, examples of which typically occurred during the periods of extreme symptoms I call returns. It was during these as the diary entries record that it becomes evident that raw child and Rebel were but parts of the same child personality. Effectively then, my timid and conforming raw child is in fact terrified of his own rebellious and angry nature. That this anger is still his, despite that fear is revealed via the last few diary entries, where the intrusive anger normally associated with Rebel now appears as belonging to the raw child himself, the boundary between them having seemingly disappeared… temporarily at least. Once again the duality within my psyche becomes apparent, the same duality that led to a particular type of childhood personality, predisposed me to breakdown when I left school and later had me considered of deserving the label OCD. But what caused such a young child to initially divide up in this way and so produce the inner characters that I and now you, reader, know so well. Well before that final insight there is one last step of self-understanding I wish the reader to explore with me, namely my personal world of dreams and especially certain significant dreams that provided that other 'window' into my mind.

Chapter Seven

Me in dreams

This chapter is not about general dream interpretation rather it deals with my dreams over a period of some years, a number of which proved to be significant in my quest for self-understanding; it is from those dreams that I have drawn the examples used in this chapter. When in analysis part of one's homework between sessions is to record any dreams to be discussed next time. Of course to prove your commitment and dedication to your analyst you naturally want to conjure up a profound and interesting dream each time... something worthy of a patient in analysis. But one soon learns that even though a construction of your own mind, a dream cannot be influenced in its subject matter or indeed when it's going to appear. That's one of the drawbacks to dreams as a therapeutic aid; they are not at all predicable. Another limitation at least initially is that to be able to use them as a source of inner information… one must be able to interpret them, and to achieve that… you must know yourself, after all it's your dream and therefore you hold the key to it. True, your analyst can help for they have hopefully discussed many dreams before, but of little use I believe are those popular books on universal dream symbolism, for even if one shares the same cultural background as the book, a particular dream symbol represented personally in your dream may or may not have the fixed meaning attributed to it. A more fundamental obstacle to easy interpretation is due to the fact that dreams tell their story in pictures… in the form of an internal drama if you like, in which the sleeping individual is both in the audience and in one form or another also on the stage. But when a dream is later remembered and subjected to rational examination, the very act of this reduces the imagery to words in which form, a lot of the subtle visual symbolism may be lost. This is doubly so when trying to share a dream with others for the written record is their only exposure to it, and is in some way akin to only having the script of a play rather than watching the play itself… it's bound to be a poor alternative. Nevertheless, reader, as you cannot enter my mental world directly, which believe me is lucky for you, my written records must serve as best they can. Of course some dreams are simple enough even for the most rudimentary attempt at translation, for example once during a period where I had to choose between two jobs one more challenging for the timid fearful me than the other, I had a dream about looking after a large safe and it proved to be a very boring job indeed. Now no great flash of insight is required here to see that going for 'the safe option' the dream's main message, was perhaps not the best choice for me. The dream symbolism here by which the imagery of the dream comes to represent both the word 'safe' and the idea of 'playing it safe' is in this case very easy to follow and indeed many dream symbols are of that nature, and will be present in the dream examples that follow.

So considering the above difficulties often in analysis a dream is only understood or appreciated fully when insights from other work have made that possible, although equally sometimes a dream will initiate new or challenge existing views about oneself that are later proven right. I've come to believe that despite their limitations dreams are another route to deeper self-understanding, and the main reason for this is that in general they come from the totality of the psyche, in other words from both conscious and unconscious areas. Therefore, the material portrayed in the dream represents aspects of oneself known and unknown. Now the unknown offers a vast repository from which the dream may draw, and thus the final dream drama may depict memories long lost since our early childhood, or represent dissociated parts of our personality, or in theory even reveal aspects of ourselves that have never been developed enough or active enough, to fall within the inner eye of consciousness. That's why dreams frequently show us behaving in ways, which are totally opposite to our consciously held attitudes and intentions, and however much this may disturb us, the dream nevertheless remains ours, it depicts us how we really are in totality… beyond the narrow confines of consciousness. Now just sometimes in that mass of material areas will be touched upon that during wakefulness produce the symptoms of a mental disorder, in my case the intrusions characteristic of OCD. Or perhaps the underlying personality traits associated with the origin or perpetuation of a disorder, become the theme of a dream. Either way, when and if this occurs such dreams can be an important source of understanding of the underlying dynamics of symptoms and their relationship to the individual concerned. Anyway enough theory as usual I hope to prove my point via actual examples… in this case a number of personal dreams together with their interpretations. I will start with dreams that provide an insight into my personality structure, as before additional words or notes added now to the original records in order to assist the reader's understanding are contained within brackets thus […].

22nd February 1984

I seem to be younger and back at school or full-time college. I'm having a great time at school; everybody knows me and likes me. Then I put on some big red shiny boots, I love these boots and feel very big and proud in them. [Next] there is a sort of internal election of certain students [about to begin] and I've been given the job of organizing it and I'm thoroughly enjoying it. A teacher asks me to give an election speech and I at once jump up on a desk and deliver a short talk to the class. [While doing this] I notice an old school friend and try to get him to notice me… but he doesn't, [in general] there's a lot of laugher and banter among the class mostly about sex. But all the time I'm only aware of my big shiny boots.

Now I wanted to start with a simple dream and this is a good example, we see me represented in a school situation in a confident and assertive manner, in stark contrast to how I really was in such situations (see chapters one & two). But the dream shows the opposite, a show-off me that in normal waking life could never find expression because I'm so timid and afraid of other peoples' reactions, but nevertheless it is a part of me I recognise and indeed has sometimes found expression via Rebel, who remember always does the opposite to the conforming me. Of course the dream symbolism goes on to show that this excessive pride in myself is hollow and too extreme, in fact it depicts me as looking silly, for I am too big for my boots… despite them being very big boots indeed. Now the next dream has a very similar theme but with one main difference, this time both sides of my personality are represented.

5th June 1985

The dream starts with me going to buy a ticket from a railway station; I am very well dressed in a new school uniform. My new blazer has in addition to the very big and shiny school badge a set of military like ribbons arranged across the chest, [making] me feel very proud about the way I look. I march up to the ticket office and on looking down I recognise the man in the booking office as one of the instructors from the training *centre [I worked as an electrical instructor at a training centre for two and half years during the eighties]* 'you look very smart Bruce', he says as he gives me my ticket. Next my train trip seems to be over and I'm now outside my old high school, it suddenly occurs to me that I have to go back for one more year… good, I say to myself I'm ready. So still wearing my wonderful new uniform with the addition of sunglasses I march into the school. It isn't until I'm right inside that I suddenly feel a bit worried about the way I have just entered, in case it has upset some of the other boys and they might come after me.

In me a journey such as the train trip of this dream, is about moving on, changing track or escaping from a situation, in this case the metaphorical journey returns me back once more to school. My wonderful new uniform again represents my new found confidence and underlying show-off nature, just as the boots did of the last dream. Equipped with these attributes I actually look forward to returning to school, to finish the year I missed in reality by leaving early. But unfortunately my bravado doesn't last… it is as shallow as my flashy uniform, which by its nature is only temporary facade and hence once back in school my old fears return. In the next dream the use of an angry persona to hide my timid disposition is the dream's main symbolic element; in a way I play at being aggressive in order to hide my fearful nature.

1984 approx.

I find myself back at my old high school in one of the main toilet blocks; there is a feeling of fear all around me. I go to a mirror over a washbasin and carefully while using the mirror as an aid, fit some fierce looking animal type teeth into my mouth. Suddenly another boy enters the toilet he doesn't appear to see me, at once I become fearful in case I attack him. But I don't have time to worry about it for long, as two more boys join us, they are much more tough and aggressive looking than the first, and I immediately remove my fierce teeth in fear of them [the boys]. Then quite suddenly I seem to be just an ordinary workman there to fix the lights, hence I have to replace a light bulb in front of the boys, who all watch me and poke fun at me… I feel so small.

This short dream deals with quite a lot, it opens by reminding me of the fear I felt at school, it's all around me in this dream and I can't escape it. But I do respond to it and try to look tough and frightening via the use of the symbolic fierce teeth. But even this childlike attempt to stand up for myself scares me… I'm reminded of the fear

I have for my own anger, just as in waking life I fear my violent intrusive thoughts. Once again like the last dream my boldness is only superficial for as soon as I remove my fierce teeth, I revert back to my normal state of the timid and anxious adult.

Another series of dreams that were very common during the early part of my analysis were what I was to eventually call my 'searching in shops' dreams. The first example given here is a very simple initial version of such a dream.

2nd October 1984

I find myself on holiday and with my father I visit a large toy and model shop. We both look around for something to buy; I look first at children's toys then move on to toys and models for older children. Next my attention is drawn to adult models and lastly to books of all different subjects (science, philosophy, history etc.). We both seem to be there for hours... but I never do find what I'm looking for.

There is a self-evident progression shown here with the symbolic move from toys to books representing the growth (or need for growth) from child to adult. So most of the dream is concerned about moving on and leaving the past behind, but the last part when I look through the various books also relates to those adult questions that confront us all, namely what should I do and what is life for? These profound questions remain unanswered for I never do find what I'm looking for. But why should I have a dream about growing up, well there is of course I'm sure the reader will agree, a marked immaturity within me. For the early environment that predisposed me to the symptoms later labelled as OCD also distorted my personality development. I appeared to grow up but behind the rational, intellectual façade, my emotional core always under the influence of my raw child aspect, never matured. Thus I developed a pseudo- maturity that was adequate to get me by while still at school, but failed dramatically when I left at 15. The next dream has the same shop theme but is a little more complex in its symbolic representation of my inability to grow up.

15th October 1982
I seem to be in a toyshop and just like a child I'm looking around at all the toys, especially some model kits. There is a pregnant woman in the shop also and with her is a small child about 5 or 6 years old, suddenly this woman has to go into hospital and the child is left behind. While I continue to choose what model I want this little child keeps hanging around me trying to attract my attention, I don't really want to know and so ignoring him I continue my search. But he doesn't give up which leaves me feeling rather embarrassed, eventually he says hello, forcing me to say hello in reply. It is then that he starts banging a toy car he has against the shop counter causing me to say, you'd better not do that! He takes little notice, eventually answering with the statement 'why it's my

car'. I then notice that the shop assistant is watching me...
I get the feeling she thinks I'm too old to be looking at
and buying toys, so I pretend the model I'm buying is
really for the little boy. When I take this to the counter the
shop assistant who seems to know all about the little boy's
mother, tells me she's in a lot of pain.

In this dream I don't move beyond the toys and
models to more mature interests, but instead yield to my
inner childlike nature, personified in this dream as the
small child who won't leave the adult me alone. Under his
influence I remain looking at the toys, which embarrasses
the adult me so much, that I have to act as if I'm buying
for him, which of course in some ways is true but not
wholly so... for partly I am excusing the immaturity of
the adult me by hiding behind the needs of the child. The
pregnant woman quite a common dream symbol for me
represents of course my mother and the event (my
brother's birth) that evoked the vulnerable child aspect
within my older child personality when I was 10 (see
chapter one). In addition, this symbol reminds me in
general of my mother fixed nature, a characteristic that is
emphasised in the storyline of the next dream, the final
example here of this type of shop dream.

1st November 1984

I decide to walk down to a nearby village to buy myself
something, on arriving I find the few shops that are full of
people, so I join the queue in one of them... I don't mind

this at all and just wait my turn. In the line just in front of me there is a young man with an older woman, who appears to be his mother but of this I'm not sure for she has always got her back to me. But whoever she is… this woman is all over this young man, monitoring and controlling him, telling him what to buy and what to do next. When it is the young man's turn to be served, his mother goes outside to wait for him. Without her he seems to be slow and indecisive and the man serving him begins to lose his temper. Finally, he does choose what he wants only to then discover he has no money and so has to go out and ask his mother for some. While he is gone I'm served and I decide on two cakes which I point out, even so I'm given different ones, which I quietly refuse and indicate again the ones I want. All through this exchange the shop assistance remains very decent towards me, eventually I'm given the correct cakes, which once paid for I leave the shop happily.

Although this dream again lacks the progression or potential progression from toys to more adult interests, the shop scenario nevertheless leads me to believe that it is once again concerned with moving on and growing up, and indeed the other elements present confirm this. As in the last example there are two aspects of me portrayed within the dream drama, the mother fixed, timid and indecisive young man and the more independent and confident me… characteristics which of course I readily recognise. The dream unequivocally shows the difference between the two, the immature young man fails to deal with life without his mother's presence, while the confident me remains in control throughout and is happy. Almost as a warning the dream shows the consequences of each life position and by way of example offers me the choice between them. This dream like the others draws upon the duality within my personality for its subject matter, and although dating from 1984 what it represents remains true, for the adult me remains largely under the influence of my raw child complex, and not only due to the symptoms this generates, but also because the very presence of this aspect, tends to undermine my adult personality... keeping me dependent and over sensitive.

Not all dreams of note appeared as part of a series some single dreams proved to be very significant as well, in fact the next example is probably the most important dream in the context of self-understanding I've ever had... dealing as it does with core aspects of my disorder and its origins. When this dream occurred early on in analysis I was unable to fully appreciated the insights the internal drama offered, this was similar to the lack of understanding I initially had of my symptoms, only after I had begun to make sense of my internal psychodynamics was I in a position to comprehend adequately the meaning of both dreams and symptoms. As I have analysed this dream many times it is offered here as an example of what may be obtained from a detailed dream interpretation.

5th September 1982

My mother was going away abroad, I just couldn't believe this or stand it as I would be left all alone, [in this dream] I was both adult and child. [Next] my mother and father and I were out buying things for her journey, I was carrying some of them when suddenly I just couldn't stand the thought of her going, so I threw down the things I was carrying. Then I threw away a little present she had given me in a [fit of] terrible anger and feeling of loss... what could I do if she goes, it was like being in the middle of a child's tantrum. [*Note made at the time:* there's something about this part that seems like an actual memory]. [Next] I was up a tree crying but when other people passed by I would try to hide the fact that I was, a lot of it was an act to get my mother to stay... my father had no time for me. Later at home I was still in a turmoil of feelings and my mother got angrier with me for breaking her present. So the more I become frustrated about her leaving the more she got angry... what could I do!

[Later] my brother came in carrying the wooden cross *[Mother's present]* my mother had given me... the one I'd thrown and broken, he said to me 'do you want this?' I did so much but I replied I didn't because my mother was there... just to show her [how I felt]. That made my mother even more angry and she shouted, 'look at that... and I bought him that... etc.

At the same time my wife was also leaving to go [abroad] on holiday, I had tantrums [in the dream] about

194

that too. [*Note made at the time:* my wife leaving me evoked the same feelings as my mother leaving].

But why is this dream so important? Well most of the elements that emerge in the dream drama also appear in symptoms or as odd tendencies while I'm awake. This indicates to me that both dream and symptoms originate from the same inner source, making the dream a useful reference for additional information on my symptoms. These 'dual' elements are as follows, those who have read the preceding chapters will remember them initially described in their everyday context:

a) In the dream drama I am cast as both adult and child, the child acts out his part while the adult me looks on. No better pictorial representation of how I am in waking life (an adult besieged by active child complexes) could I believe be asked for.

b) Sudden intrusive impulses/ images of me throwing something down in anger and despair are the waking equivalent to the action within the dream… when I throw down my mother's things and then throw away her present to me.

c) Similar to (b) is the intrusive impulse/ image to break the things I really want, which is a Rebel opposite/ contrary tendency when awake. Also the linked but contrasting feeling of only having a broken little thing, which is nevertheless very important to me…. a sentiment that very often appears when my raw child is close. These two waking experiences naturally relate to the dream in the following ways, firstly the throwing down of the present which breaks... is obviously in the context of the dream, 'breaking what I really want'. This oppositional tendency appears again although in a slightly more complex form, when I refuse to take the broken present back, although I want so much. Secondly of course the broken present has associations with my raw child's feelings of only having a broken thing that is nevertheless important, in the dream's case because it comes from Mother.

d) The general theme throughout the dream is one of ambivalence; this is its core emotional bias. Hence I'm shown throughout the drama as being both angry with and needing my mother. Other ambivalent scenes include the throwing down of my mother's present, and the rejection of the present when it is offered back to me, each time my rage at the situation and Mother, prevents me accepting the thing I want so much... not so much the physical present as represented in the dream, but my mother's approval and unconditional love.

e) Midway through the dream I am depicted up a tree crying, this part is concerned with attention seeking and pretence. Both of these tendencies I recognize as personal characteristics and as elements present within my disorder... for I've often utilized my symptoms (when they have been at a manageable levels) to appear more interesting and/ or to attract attention. Interestingly this is one of the reasons why my OCD perpetuates, there is mixed with the undeniable suffering... a psychological gain.

Before going into more detail concerning these aspects I want to draw the reader's attention to an even more important part, the part within the dream that links my dream world with my reality. Despite its importance this appears right at the end where attention is drawn to the fact that my wife was also going on holiday and I had tantrums about that too. Now this was indeed true she really was going away at the time... so this event is the real life trigger or instigator of the dream. Knowing this link greatly assists in the dream's interpretation and the understanding of any insights within. So why would my wife's holiday trip trigger a dream all about my mother going away, well the dream itself provides the connection, as both imminent departures are shown to provoke similar childish tantrums. Thus the dream clearly demonstrates how my past influences my present, specifically here how my early relationship with my mother still determines to some extent the relationship with my wife. The dream's storyline gives insight into why I also developed symptoms at this time; for my wife's planned departure had obviously evoked old fears of abandonment originally associated with my mother. As usual these symptoms reflected the different natures of my child complexes, consequently there was anxiety and panic from my raw child, while intrusive thoughts of violence directed at my wife came from Rebel. In a way the symptoms were the waking equivalent the dream's story, but the dream is easier to understand for it provides more information, for example the internal drama reveals why I was so angry and vulnerable. This is not true of the symptoms, which in this instant were mainly sudden intrusive thoughts, as usual passively experienced... as their motivation and personal connection remains beyond one's awareness.

Considering then that the dream and the symptoms share a common source namely an emotional charged fear of being abandoned by Mother, what is the nature of this source and why is present within me. Again the dream itself assists here suggesting by its feel and content that it is based upon a real memory, this conviction of reality is rare in my dreams and perhaps has appeared only twice in the hundreds of dreams I've recorded. I now believe that because of its parallels to waking symptomatology and this 'actual memory' feeling, that this dream emanates from and represents an important event from my past... an event that is of great significance to the natures of my child complexes. With its emphasis on Mother leaving me, something, which as far as I know never took place, the only alternative is that the dream relates to the time when I was forced to leave her, and this is most likely to be my visit to hospital in 1959 when I was approximately 2 ½ years old. To a small child it is never they who leave Mother it is always the other way round, so when I found myself alone in the hospital... Mother had abandoned me! As mentioned before this occurrence was my first confirmation that I was bad and no longer Mother's special little boy, and hence this hospital experience was viewed as a punishment. Nevertheless, this event, traumatic as it undoubtedly was, did not cause my OCD, but it did greatly determine the way it manifested itself especially during the earlier years when compulsions dominated, for these were clearly all about fears of illness and of going to hospital as a punishment (see chapter one).

So it would seem that both dream and associated symptoms share a common origin…a traumatic event from my past, and this forms an active source powerful enough to produce waking intrusions a common feature of my OCD, plus a dream that contains these same aspects within a personal drama. Self-evidently then understanding the dream's narrative, I'm sure the reader will agree, offers an opportunity to understand the nature of the mental functioning beneath these symptoms. Thus although triggered by my wife going on holiday without me, the dream confirms that the feelings evoked were originally linked to, and remain associated with my mother, that is why they felt at odds with and out of proportion to the adult viewed situation. The result was an inner conflict between the adult rational me and my long-standing child aspects within, which made their presence known via the symptoms I endured, and in this instant the dream I experienced. But these symptoms didn't just appear in relation to this trigger they have been common occurrences throughout my disorder's history, this makes fully understanding the dream even more crucial, if it is perhaps capable of illuminating the general 'characteristics' of my child complexes. For example, as mentioned earlier the tendency within me appearing either as an intrusive impulse to throw down any gift in anger, (see chapter six) or the same in a more subtle adult guise, the propensity to reject things I really want… especially if others can witness me doing this. Within the dream drama this tendency is shown clearly linked to my mother, it is her present I throw down in anger and later reject again. Thus what the dream shows is the prototype reaction on which all subsequent similar impulses are based, along with the significant individual they were originally directed at. Obviously other symptoms with equally long histories such as the urge to, 'break what I really want' and the emotionally charged idea, 'of only having a broken little thing' are similarly linked, as may be inferred from the dream's storyline, hence they too appear to have their origins in my early relationship with my mother.

More fundamentally the dream shows plainly the essential duality of my child personality (by duality I mean here the tendency to be either 'passive/ fearful' or 'angry/ active') for there is rage and fear present, together with frustration and need, and most importantly underlying these there is love and hate. But crucially this is love and more importantly hate directed at an individual I also desperately needed and loved, this caused an

200

internal conflict that was intolerable to bear. It was then I believe that my timid, anxious and dependent child could no longer deal with such anger, and to maintain the image of being Mother's special little boy this anger was denied and withdrawn from, only to be taken up by Rebel an already defiant and oppositional part of me. He, Rebel carries the anger my raw child could not. When one looks at my later symptoms the same duality is clear to see, for my raw child finds expression via compulsions to check, in sudden paranoid fears and in the need to be a pleaser, while intrusions from Rebel reflect his anger, defiance and oppositional nature. These two now largely hidden aspects of me are I am sure shown in this dream that is itself a caricature of my original relationship with Mother. But I state again this one example is not the cause or source of my OCD, it is but one small window into the nature of that relationship. In me the predisposition to later develop this disorder, originates I believe in the super close and overprotected relationship I had with my anxious and vulnerable mother. Within this exclusive relationship that dominated the first four years of my life, the inclination for later OCD was progressively and insidiously formed.

The next dream to be mentioned although dreamt many years later is nevertheless similar to the last in the nature of the elements present and its meaning. It thus demonstrates once more just how much my relationship with my wife remains influenced by my past relationship with Mother.

4th May 1995

This dream starts with the knowledge that my wife is going away; in fact, she is going to marry someone else. The whole of the dream is filled with a turmoil of feelings, [alternating around] a mix of anger and sadness. The last scene [shows] my wife still angry at me and leaving, so I rush into the bedroom where she is and bury my head in her lap [she is sitting on the bed] and say I'm sorry and beg her not to go away... and she doesn't.

Although my mother does not appear in this dream the way I am shown responding to my wife's impending departure is distinctly childlike, while the turmoil of feelings has the same emotional feel as the obviously infantile tantrum of the previous dream drama. Anger directed at or associated with my mother such as that in the earlier dream has, as the reader will well know by now a long history in me, appearing as it does both in symptoms and dreams alike. Indeed, I have come to believe that the anger that spontaneously appeared at the age of 15 when I felt rejected by my mother, forms now the independent source of rage that Rebel draws upon for his angry and violent intrusions. The following two dream examples show this reserve of anger finding expression via my mother.

12th July1982

You *[Dr Cutner my analyst]* and I were both at my home sitting in the living room, we were talking and I was reading from this book *[one of my note books I took to sessions]*. My mother joined us from the kitchen, she stood over us trying to listen to our conversation and read my notes. She got very upset about it all… at which point you *[Dr Cutner]* seemed to disappear. Alone now with my mother she went on and on about something, in the end I lost my temper and shouted at her, I will bloody kill you. Unperturbed, she carried on… now going on about how I shouldn't speak to her like that or say such things. Then the thought entered my mind that I might kill her as I'm ill, [i.e. having intrusive thoughts of violence] Mother then advances towards me still ranting on and I shout, keep back, keep back but she still keeps coming right up close. [Despite this] I know I have full control, even though I'm very angry, I just push her to one side and walk to the other side of the room. Nevertheless, Mother doesn't stop, she is still going on about how terrible it all is. My father, who had been standing there all this time but saying and doing nothing, suddenly spoke up and said you've been going on for two hours now! Taking the opportunity to Speak up for myself I say it was all her fault, and warn her again to keep away from me. I asked my father if this was not true but he didn't want to say, in the end I just walked out of the house.

This dream is one of the many I discussed with Dr Cutner during my analysis. At the time I was exploring the period when I run back home from my first job, that period of extreme anxiety and dependency the outcome of which was the appearance of my Rebel type intrusions, and assuredly this dream is about that time. I know this for certain because it contains the words directed at my mother then, by my father, namely 'you've been going on for two hours now' it was said in response to one of Mother's long tirades about me being at home and not working etc. So having confirmed its subject matter what else does this dream show of that phase in my life. Well the general tense and strained atmosphere at home or at least the way I perceived it at the time is well illustrated. In fact, most of the dream is a parody of my mother's constant preoccupation with why I wasn't working, with its moral emphasis and fear of what other people might think. This situation had in reality fuelled the growing animosity between us and led eventually to the terrible arguments that typified this period. The resentment I felt at this 'betrayal' seemed to release an extreme anger that surprised even me, let alone my mother, and it was this anger that found verbal expression in the vehement shouting at my mother that I hated her (see chapter two). Interestingly my fear of my anger, a direct import from my constant waking fears at this time is shown to be unfounded, for the dream drama presents me maintaining full control throughout. This portrayal so opposite of my waking fears has appeared in many dreams, indicating I feel that in general my anxious scrutiny of myself was in reality somewhat unjustified. The dream continues showing yet another aspect... my father's indifference. In stark contrast to my mother's agitation he preferred a more distant and unemotional response, and indeed had to be pushed by Mother into getting involved in my plight. This stance being I must say entirely consistent with his personality, for I never knew him talk personally or emotionally at any meaningful depth with anyone. The introduction to the dream refers to one other detail and although it is not related to the period the rest of the drama is set, it does reflect important feelings relevant at the time the dream was dreamt. This was my mother's animosity and unease at my decision to undergo analysis, it was as if she feared she would be found at fault or somehow implicated when the cause of my disorder was discovered. She never seemed able to accept that the process was about understanding rather than blame.

Now the next dream again portrays me in a situation where there is great anger at my mother, but this example is drawn from earlier memories.

July 1982

My mother and I are both in the sitting room at home *[my childhood home]* the room is like it was many years before. Next my mother is sitting down and I am standing in front of her she is talking to me... asking me something, she says, are you prepared to give your bed up? I reply that I'm not... at which point she becomes all hurt and angry and tries to make me feel very guilty so that I will change my mind, but I won't. Whatever she says and however much I feel guilty I won't change my mind, I just won't. [Suddenly] I jump at her and grab her by the throat and try and strangle her.

Powerful stuff indeed... the strength of my anger represented here leaves nothing to the imagination, but what had evoked such a violent reaction. Well the dream shows the living room as it was in the mid 1960s, thus the child me who stands before my mother would be about 9 or 10 years old. On initially reading of this dream I had immediately and spontaneously recalled some real events of that time of which I'm sure the dream alludes. These events were associated with my grandparents on my mother's side, when they came to stay [we lived with my other grandparents permanently] the only place for them to sleep was my room, hence the question as portrayed in the dream drama. The trouble was one couldn't just refuse or offer up some acceptable excuse with Mother, or expect a one off argument or punishment. For in such a situation anything other than a quick positive response would see her aggrieved and upset as if one had fallen from some expected standard, and so were no longer her special little boy. In short, my mother had the tendency to use the withdrawal of love as a punishment... by tendency I mean I don't think she deliberately set out to do this or even considered or reflected upon it, rather it was just her natural way of responding. But as a relational strategy it tends to make one feel guilty and powerless while over time resentment and thus anger sets in… anger, or perhaps in the end more accurately rage, that in the dream is represented in a physical manner.

Earlier when discussing the dream concerning my mother leaving me, I connected the dream's storyline with the real life event my early hospital visit and I believe the following dream specifically deals with that traumatic episode. It is indeed a rare dream for over the period I've recorded dreams, there has only been two others with similar subject matter.

From 1982
All of a sudden I'm in hospital [as an adult] and I don't know why. There are a lot of people around and [apparently] I'm in for an operation. Next I'm in a wheelchair talking to some other patients one of whom says to me, 'you won't be able to go to the toilet after that'. Next I seem to be waking up after the operation I feel no pain, only a strange feeling around the top of my legs as if I'm wrapped up tight there. Once again I go around in my wheelchair when suddenly I see that my brother is there [as a very small child] apparently he has had the same operation as me. [Then] I get a strange feeling something went wrong in his operation, the same idea also occurs about mine. I'm taking him around the hospital when I meet a nurse; she says in a loud voice, 'he's the one… he's nothing now, not a boy nor a girl'. At these remarks I lose my temper with her, and in order to

protect my brother I threaten her with all sorts of things if she doesn't stop talking like that, at which point she just walks off laughing. Later back at home with my mother I am very angry with her as well, and I say to her, 'why didn't you tell me what would happen to Keith, [i.e. *my brother*] why did I have to find out that way!'

This dream although recorded was left unused and without an interpretation for at least 25 years, for although I felt I knew what it alluded to I wasn't adequately sure. It was not until my mother in one of her unguarded moments was speaking about my circumcision that an actual connection between that event and the dream emerged. For she mentioned that after the operation I was wrapped up tight around the groin area, thus with its subject matter confirmed the rest of the dream yielded to understanding. Although I am shown as an adult going into hospital the same is clearly happening to a small child, in this case my brother plays this child even though he was already 15 in 1982…so why then did he appear in this role rather than a younger me? Well I could offer up various psychoanalytical reasons, such as the symbolic substitution enabled the trauma to be displaced, and thus viewed more distantly so reducing anxiety, or perhaps a resentful part of me just wanted him to suffer as I did. In fact, I feel the reason is much less complex. My brother Keith was the last born into the family and thus was always regarded as a child, and indeed in common with many others so born, he was typically known as babe well beyond when that was appropriate. So being our family's archetypal child it was he who portrayed the child in my dream drama, but whatever the 'mask' the child who has the operation is undoubtedly me, for it is my story and like the 'mother leaving me dream', I appear as both adult and child in it.

Now the reader I'm sure will have noticed two symbolic references to something having happened to my genitals, well saying symbolic is a bit pretentious really as the dream's approach is more comedy innuendo. No one could mistake the intended association of the other patient's warning or the nurse's mocking comments... this dream is all about circumcision. Other important elements that touch upon how I reacted to the real event include the general anxiety present, plus the uncertain fear that something might have gone wrong. More significantly (in relation to my OCD) is the intense anger directed at my mother at the end of the dream, which is linked to the concluding words, why did I have to find out that way! This reveals both how unprepared I was and how much at the time I blamed my mother for what had happened. Again in an unguarded moment many years later my mother stated (although she has denied saying it ever since) that on returning from hospital I had refused to talk for a few days, I feel the anger and bitterness touched upon in this dream may well account for that behaviour. The next dream is a variation of the last and while not so well defined and understandable it clearly shares the same theme.

2nd January 1984

I am in hospital... I seem to be a child again. I am lying in what appears to be a very high-sided bath; I seem to be right at the bottom of this looking up with the high sides all around me. The bath is located at the end of a hospital bed and my parents are there with me sitting on this bed. There is another bed besides mine on which there is another boy. At first I'm not frightened... I just wonder why I am here. Then it dawns on me that I must be having an operation, but [apparently] I will only be in the hospital a short time. Next I notice a male nurse going over to the boy next to me, I hear him speak to the boy saying 'that's a big one!' Then this nurse comes over and says exactly the same to me as I lie in the bath naked... I feel very embarrassed. [Next] shockingly the nurse then bends down and takes my penis in his hand, I sit up quickly and at the same time I hear my father say to my mother, 'they do that to get them up.'

This dream is one of perhaps a group of two or three that had at the end an internal call to take notice of what had just been dreamt. The following note made at the time recorded this: (this dream was brought to my attention by the words at the end... remember this dream it is important, remember this dream it is important!)

Knowing I always looked to my dreams with the hope that one would provide that key insight I always longed for, why was this dream considered important enough to warrant such a remark. Well the internal statement that it is to be remembered seems to imply importance, either because the dream contains information previously outside my conscious awareness or because it helps explains information available to me, but as yet not fully appreciated. So what important elements are present well it appears similar to the other hospital dream, namely I am at first confused not knowing why I'm there, later I become aware that I am to have an operation and the same sort of almost crude references call attention to the nature of this operation. But there are some differences also for here I am depicted directly as the child undergoing the trauma, and the state of being a child is confirmed within the dream by the nature of my perception of the things around me, such as the very large bath. I should perhaps at this point note again that this feeling of being small in a big world also occurs then I'm under the influence of my raw child aspect as a symptom in normal waking life. Also clearly present within this dream is the feeling of menace and fear in regard to the medical staff and my shock and embarrassment at the examination, these must be depictions of how I really felt at the time. In addition, although my parents are shown as being nearby they are passive neither supporting nor comforting me, this reflects the reality of the event because of course they weren't there... I faced this trauma alone. But why was this dream

211

flagged up as important to remember, I think now not for any particulate reason, rather its importance lays in its general representation of an event that has some aetiological significance in nature of my OCD.

The characteristics of my raw child aspect should by now be well known to the reader, pure representations of this child have been unusual in my dreams, nevertheless some do exist and the following are two examples chosen for this chapter are particularly interesting because of the distinctive manner this inner child has been portrayed within them.

10th December 1984
The dream starts when I pay a visit to Woolworth's [the shop] here I meet a doctor who tells me about a little girl he has just about given up [trying to help]. [Apparently] she just can't face the world anymore I am told and spends all her time hiding in the shop refusing to speak or see anybody. I ask where the little girl is and the doctor points to under one of the counters, getting down on my hands and knees I try to see where she is but it is dark and difficult to make out anything. Then suddenly with the help of the doctor I just make out her little head moving. She seems to me to be behind a sort of grille, which I am just able to see through; strangely it all reminds me of a church confessional box. As soon as I go near to her the little girl cries out, go away, go away, don't come near me please... I'm frightened! I want to help you I reply, I will

just stay here and talk. At first it is very difficult to get any response from the girl all she will say is how frightened she is of the big world outside and so prefers to hide away. I continue [by] saying you can't live here all your life... don't waste your life like this, there's so much to do and see out in the world... if you take my hand and come with me I'll show you. The little girl still won't move but I keep on trying, please come with me, I was like you once but now I can face the world and you will be able to as well. Then slowly the girl moves out from behind the counter, I look back at the doctor who has stayed to watch, I can see by the look on his face that he can hardly believe what's happening. [Next] holding her hand carefully I take the girl all around the shop showing her all the different counters in turn. Then when she appears to have lost some of her original fear I even take her outside, but I soon discover she has no shoes on and so I must carry her back. Once inside I tell her that's enough for one day and that I will return tomorrow to see her again, at that [remark] she runs off happily into the shop. [Later alone] I think to myself what a wonderful thing I have done... but no that seems far too big headed...rather it is perhaps through me that something has stirred in her, which will lead to her own salvation. There is a general feeling of wonder almost spiritual in nature linked to this little girl's loss of fear. I imagine myself returning again and again spending my whole life if necessary in order to set her completely free.

From a psychoanalytical perspective this is a very positive dream for it represents the first tentative steps towards the synthesis of two different aspects of my psyche. Under the watchful gaze of the doctor the adult me is seen reaching out to and eventually embracing an infantile part of myself. In essence this fusion between aspects of oneself that before were effectively outside one's awareness is the ultimate objective of the psychodynamic approach. All the striving to understand and gain deeper insight in one's symptoms, dreams and other traits of personality are really all to that end... that is the final part of the healing process. Luckily there are gains along the way, for I unfortunately have never been able to achieve this final resolution. My infantile complexes remain despite my insights stubbornly autonomous, certainly remaining beyond my conscious influence and to an extent even now, beyond my full understanding; consequently, they remain the source of my symptoms and thus my OCD continues. Interestingly, this dream depicts my raw child aspect who to me in normal waking life appears male as a little girl; why did the dream drama choose a change in gender... well I believe it is to emphasize this child's sensitivity and timidity, so the dream states he is more like a girl than a boy. Now this is not my psyche's attempt at being controversial or a wish to offend women, for I wouldn't choose to use such symbolism at a conscious, rational level. Rather it is merely the way different factors within my personality, some conscious others not, have conspired to represent my raw child aspect, and of course a dream is normally only for one's internal consumption. Also interesting and perhaps more difficult to dismiss is the fact my dream plumps for a male doctor image to represent my female analyst... now that can't have pleased her. To be different here I am going to use the original write up/ interpretation as read to Dr Cutner on the 18th December 1984, the actual dream (devoid of interpretation) would have been discussed the session before. Reading through it now it does seem rather naïve but even so it basically says what I would currently detail, and besides it provides the reader with a direct example of my 'dream work' while in analysis.

December, 1984

This dream set as it is in Woolworth's [starts] like the many other dreams I have of shops. But instead of looking from counter to counter, from shelf to shelf for something I never seem to make my mind up about buying, *[a reference to my typical shop dreams]* here a doctor figure tells me about a little girl so afraid of the world that she never leaves the shop. Perhaps she was what I was looking for in the other dreams, a part of me no doubt as we agreed last time, *[the previous session]* a frightened, sensitive and childish part... a part that now seems it is time to help and comfort. There is a powerful feeling throughout that this child should not miss out on the wonders of the world, it is for me to help her overcome her fears. To that end I take her hand *[the dream's representation of the process of synthesis]* and show her the world just beyond the shop. The dream shows she isn't quite ready to go very far yet by the fact she has no shoes, this requires me to carry her back. Even so I leave her feeling more confident intending to return the next day to take her further. As we said last time this is a very positive dream not because the aspect of me represented by the girl was unknown previously to me, but because the dream reveals the possibility of her losing her fear under the protection of my more adult side, and eventually joining with me in the future *[in other words this child element grows up]*. This possibility being very important in a person such as I who suffers from many childlike fears that limit adult life, and in addition there is of course the gain to the rest of the personality she brings with her, and we spoke of this being represented in the dream by the powerful emotional nature of its ending.

From this interpretation it is obvious that the prospect of my raw child complex integrating with my adult personality was viewed as the most important message of this dream. This possibility being considered beneficial in theory because firstly there would be a reduction in symptoms, after all intrusive thoughts cannot suddenly appear in one's awareness if their origin also lies within one's consciousness, and secondly such dissociated complexes withhold from the main personality the mental functioning and emotion isolated within them. These in normal circumstances would have formed part of the repertoire of thoughts and feelings available to the personality as a whole. So when integration occurs these qualities become available to enrich and broaden the individual's personality, it is of this phenomenon that the end of the dream's interpretation refers too. But as I have stated before this final act of fusion never took place in me, there are many reasons for this, for OCD is a complex and heterogeneous disorder that operates on many levels. My OCD tends to perpetuate for within its symptoms and limitations on my life, there is obscured but nevertheless present a gain to my overall personality. This has been difficult to accept or even acknowledge during the periods when I have been plagued with intrusions and suffered high levels of anxiety, but it remains true. The nature of this gain like the disorder itself is complex, both developed in the period of turmoil that followed my leaving school. Basically within the different symptoms and their interaction with me there was a measured expression of deeply held needs and a compromise between contradictory desires, thus in a strange way the disorder partly served as a way of continuing beyond my breakdown, it was a new way of getting by... but at the cost of being forever ill. I will return to this curious feature of OCD in the last chapter.

The very last example here of dream related material is both a recount of a dream and its interpretation combined just as it was read to Dr Cutner in 1985, its subject matter dealing as it does with my raw child is similar in meaning to the last dream. It contains a reference to a once well-known actor, Jack Warner although I'm sure some reading this book now won't know him, hence this note. Jack Warner (1895-1981) a star of music hall, radio, film and TV was perhaps best known for his role as P.C (later Sgt) Dixon in TV police series Dixon of Dock Green, and it is as this character that he appears in my dream. The persona of this character, which also became personally associated with the actor, was one of scrupulous honesty, firmness and fairness and with these attributes he came to represent the ideal father figure, and indeed in my dream that's what he portrays. However, if asked at the time to consciously consider a person suitable for such a label I would not of thought of Jack Warner… it is strange how these collective cultural notions are automatically absorbed only crossing into my awareness, in this example via a dream.

26th February 1985

Last week I had a dream in which a little girl had been rescued from a very dark house where she had been kept prisoner by a wicked old man for many years. The old man had first been arrested and then the little girl was led out into the light of day by a very kind policeman based on the character played by Jack Warner. She was first taken to a bakery where the policeman offers to buy her a large cake, but because she had been hidden away for so long she didn't seem to understand what the cake was for. Eventually with much coaxing she understood it was something good to eat and accepted it gladly. [Later] she was taken to the police station where everyone was very kind to her and seemed willing to help in every possible way.

[Note at the time continues]

even though I could hardly remember this dream's details, there was a great feeling of breaking out... of freedom, shown in the dream's [pictorial depiction] as the escape from the dark house into the bright sunlight. Straight away I naturally felt the little girl was a part of me, a part that had remained hidden away from the world. This occurring because a wicked old man had kept her prisoner, we agreed *[Dr Cutner and I at the previous session]* that this old man could represent my father, but not only him... rather the oppressive atmosphere of the dark house symbolized the whole of my early environment. But now in this very positive dream this timid and frightened part of me comes out from suppression to join the conscious me... this being represented in the dream by her emergence into the light of day *[consciousness]* in the dream's imagery. Also a new father figure is shown taking over the important job of leading the little girl out into the world, the dream's choice here being a character I haven't thought of in years although I did watch him on TV as a child. Jack Warner is the policeman who rescues my child aspect... he is my dream's choice for the ideal father figure, and even after we had discussed his presence and you *[Dr Cutner]* had mentioned that he was often thought of in this way by many people, I still found it remarkable that this collective idea had so effectively taken hold in me, while I (the conscious me) had remained ignorant of its presence until the dream.

Once more as in the previous dream my raw child aspect is portrayed as a frightened little girl, this choice of symbolism appearing again despite the two months between the dreams. Other similarities are the dark house where the girl is trapped, which just like the shop where she hides effectively isolates her from the world, evidently these dreams tell the same story. But they tell it different ways for the second dream lacks the doctor character, while the adult me who attempts the assist the hiding child is here replaced with a universal father figure. Perhaps this means I'm not ready to take on this important role. Also there are two representations of fatherhood present one positive the other obviously negative, one helps the little girl face the world (that is of course to grow up) while the other binds her to him and prevents any such development. When this was discussed with Dr Cutner the consensus was this negative father figure could represent my actual father, although this was mitigated somewhat by the more general idea that this figure may also represent my restrictive and overprotective early environment. Father did of course appear in quite a few of my dreams both symbolically as above and in a more realistic guise, despite this the reader will have noticed by now that he doesn't feature much in this book this is because to include him would I believe only muddle an already convoluted story, and the truth is his pathological influence in regard to my predisposition to later psychological difficulties is just much less than my mother's. For me the origins of my OCD resides in this latter relationship... that is, within the complex reciprocal interplay between Mother and her problems and the way I perceived her and our relationship. It is the nature of this lived dyadic experience that I will attempt to fully clarify in the next and final chapter. Here I will end with a final mention of my father in general and in relation to the last dream; he was as stated before a rather emotionally remote man neither showing nor comfortable with the emotions of others. Thus I'm sure my over sentimental and timid raw child aspect would have both horrified and embarrassed him; he would have defiantly not embraced this aspect of me... just as indeed he would have never embraced the actual me!

In summary the intention of this chapter was to demonstrate the possibility of using dream material, as an additional tool in the understanding of the personal factors underpinning disorders such as OCD. In order not to bore the reader unduly I used only a small percentage of the many dreams I have recorded over some years, because they were considered at the time significant. For example, taking the period I was in analysis about 150 dreams fell into that category, these would have been drawn from countless others perhaps only half remembered or impossible to understand. In the planning of this book I reduced these to 40 of the most relevant to my story, and for the reason given above only 14 were finally used. My point here is to again emphasise that although dreams are generated within our own minds, because of their unpredictable and autonomous nature they are a difficult therapeutic tool to use. Often they annoyingly seem to abandon you when you're hoping for an important one to come along, and for me the truth always remained: for every useful dream there were numerous others that shunned your wishes and evaded your attempts to make sense of them. Nevertheless, I hope I have shown that when relevant dreams do occur, because they originate from both conscious and unconscious areas of the psyche they offer a real chance to gain insight into mental functioning that is usually beyond our awareness. Really useful dreams either further illuminate the personality within which the disorder operates, or just sometimes may touch upon the core issues and represent the actual symptoms themselves. If this occurs what is normally experienced via sudden intrusions may now appear in greater depth and in other forms, allowing for the possibility of new understanding. Unfortunately, the dream's largely visual medium initially makes it difficult to understand, but remember you don't need to an expert on general interpretation... after all this is your dream, and only your dreams need to be understood if you are utilizing them for personal insight. Of course someone familiar with the language of dreams is very useful, but remember not even they will be (unless they work with you for some time) an expert on your dreams. In general insight into a dream's meaning becomes easier as one gains insight into oneself overall; often this works both ways with dreams providing new insights allowing a more informed self to more accurately understand other dreams. Even if the meaning of a dream is not at once recognized keeping a written record will often begin to show certain story lines and symbols repeating as the dreams deal with reoccurring personal themes, and of course, comprehending the meaning of any one of a similar series of dreams helps to clarify them all, but only if you have bothered to record them. Also in my experience it is not necessary to understand absolutely every detail of a dream for it to prove useful, even a sense of its meaning may be enough to lead one towards greater understanding. Finally, I will affirm again my belief that despite their disadvantages dreams are worth persevering with for they have the unique ability to provide a non-contrived additional view of one's psyche, that no other treatment or technique can hope to replicate. This conviction I hope is supported by the few dream examples used here, which if my interpretations have been adequate should result in the reader being able to understand my raw child and rebel complexes, plus the personality in which they reside... just a little bit better.

Chapter Eight

Putting it all together

For me this is by far the most important chapter and it could be stated with some truth that the rest of the book exists only to support and justify the conclusions that now follow. It was always my intention to attempt to show that a case of OCD displaying all the typical diverse and elaborate symptomatology could be understood in psychodynamic terms, given the time and persistence to achieve that. As stated I believe the origins of my disorder are to be found within my personal history, and thus even current triggering events are triggers, because they evoke sensitivities formed long ago. Fundamentally my OCD edifice rests upon the complex interaction of autonomous internal mental functioning, much of which originates from my childhood and much of that initially at least, was beyond my awareness. But the book also serves another purpose that of establishing my credentials to write such a treatise in the first place, without the usual background or qualifications in psychopathology. It is my hope that the book's nature and content backed up by the numerous real life examples within it show a consistent rational approach of sufficient calibre, to convince the reader of the validity of my approach and subsequent conclusions. Also of course this story is not second-hand told via another, however well qualified, this recount represents my direct experience of OCD as unfortunately I share my mind with it...put simply I have had a ring side seat to this disorder for most of my life. It is from that perspective that I offer my insights to the reader, this and the 30 plus years of study and introspection of my own suffering, permit me I believe to be my own expert. Yes of course these insights relate to me... after all I'm the case history, but I believe they are not unique to me and many of the elements in this book will I am sure find parallels in the experience of others. Thus I hope the fundamental tenet of the book will be of interest to the many who seek understanding into this perplexing disorder, be they fellow sufferers or those who strive to treat them.

But before I continue with the underlying causes of my OCD I perhaps better describe what OCD is and here I'm not considering the usual signs and symptoms that would result in the individual receiving the label of OCD. No here I want to try to describe to the reader what it is like to experience OCD in your own head, when one's normal thinking is suddenly disrupted by other thoughts, which are strange and threatening to one's existing mental integrity. In an individual with OCD these intrusions are perceived and recognized spontaneously as thoughts however alien these thoughts appear. They do not present themselves as in some psychotic disorders as if heard from outside neither are they experienced with the built in belief that they have been 'inserted' into the mind by some external agency. I from the very first never doubted my ego-dystonic disruptions the ones that appeared when I was 15 were anything other than thoughts, however in general there are differences in the way individual sufferers perceive their symptoms, in other words the level of insight varies from person to person. A lack of insight is especially prevalent in the case of children and one might imagine that this is solely due to the critical function of reflective self-awareness being undeveloped, but it also occurs for another reason, the subject matter of the symptoms tends to be ego-syntonic in children, that is it is in keeping with the child's concept of itself, and indeed my early compulsions were all of that nature, the shock of experiencing oppositional thoughts was not present. But whatever the type of intrusion there is something strange and compelling about a thought, image or impulse you didn't consciously participate in. They seem to possess a self-importance and innate truth that is difficult to ignore, however nonsensical the individual concerned knows the unbidden material is. Of course I am aware that relatively recent studies have shown that even 'normal' people have intrusive thoughts etc. and I'm sure that is correct, but the inference often made from this insight is that the only different between individuals with OCD and the normals is the way they react to their intrusions, for example OCD sufferers are much more anxious about theirs. But as one who has experienced various intrusions for years I'm of the belief that the obsessive thoughts themselves are different, in me they were much more established and systematic, there is a consistency about them as if I harboured a different nature, which operated in parallel with my normal thinking, and of course my intrusions were clearly linked in understandable ways to trigger events in the world around me.

So to experience OCD is to become painfully aware that you…the conscious adult rational part is not the only 'voice' within your head, other thoughts and feelings abound, intruding upon normal thinking and pulling one away from reality. It is like one is at odds with oneself; an internal conflict the result of which is one's rational self is besieged from what else lurks within you. What I have just emotively described would in psychodynamic terms be portrayed as the Ego of the individual struggling with internal (largely unconscious) forces, the origins of these being either psychogenic or neuropsychological in nature or perhaps a combination of such factors. I have come to believe that there may be a number of OCD types, all manifesting themselves as above and thus producing a similar experience for the sufferer, but nevertheless having different causes and thus subtle differences in structure. For example, in early onset OCD such as mine, the underlying fears driving the obsessions tend to be more about that individual feeling vulnerable and abandoned, just like my raw child complex. While those who more typically develop the disorder in their late teens or early adulthood, have obsessional thoughts more concerned about the safety of other people, but of course it remains true that each case is unique to the sufferer concerned even if symptoms are similar. For me I am convinced that the fundamental cause of my unbidden intrusions and earlier compulsions are dissociated parts of myself. These are still active fragments of past personality that continue to communicate with my present personality, the nature of these communications representing the disposition and fixated age of these parts. In me these are infantile in nature, and being consistent and longstanding in their manner I have come to know their discrete natures, they are the timid and fearful mother fixed raw child, and the oppositional and angry Rebel, both of whom the reader should by now know well. Confrontation with these inner aspects perplexes and alarms my adult personality, firstly because of the emotional baggage they bring with them from my past, and secondly because their infantile thought patterns seem to threaten and challenge the integrity of my present thinking. But why did this dissociation occur in me that was to later predispose me to OCD, well the origins lay I believe within the complex reciprocal interplay that took between my mother and I during our rather exclusive and intense relationship that dominated my first four years, and it is to that significant period I now turn my attention.

By her own admittance my mother was naïve concerning motherhood, knowing nothing about babies… it was all new to her, for she had never been interested in babies like some girls were. But more importantly for the effect it would have upon my developing personality was her natural tendency to be anxious, this betrayed itself via a general fearfulness in certain everyday circumstances, which at one point during these formative years escalated to a period of panic attacks. It also showed itself in specific phobias, such as a fear of the dark, being alone, the cellar and rats therein at a certain house, and in marked claustrophobia. All these fears tended to intensify when she was alone, for my mother has a clear dependent personality and therefore has in order to feel safe to have people she feels she can trust around her. Deprived of this support especially in later life and particularly when subjected to other stressors (such as being ill) she can decompensate into a super dependent childlike state, characterized by high anxiety, vulnerable clingy nature and an inability to make any decisions for herself. Linked to this need for others is her propensity to be passive and subordinate in dealing with other people, in short she is a pleaser in order to ensure she isn't rejected or abandoned.

Self-assertion, self-esteem and self-belief are all sadly lacking in my mother, and of course a lifetime of being passive and continually needing to please others, has led to resentment and regret as her own needs and wishes have constantly been frustrated.

But how did Mother's state of mind affect me, well quite simply she communicated her anxiousness by being herself around me. I'm quite sure this was unintentional and probably she didn't even realize what was occurring, but for me slowly internalising her anxious state made the world appear an unpredictable and dangerous place, and this indeed is how my raw child aspect still perceives it. But more important that this process was the perception (because of her anxiousness) that Mother herself seemed vulnerable and insecure, this for an already anxious young child who was solely dependent upon its primary caregiver for a feeling of security, compounded the feeling of being unsafe. To this pathological mix yet another dimension must be added that of my mother's neurotic personality in general and the way this manifested itself. Such people and of course I should know for I am one, are wrapped up in their own internal problems, which although perhaps not explicitly expressed, nevertheless influence and determine their interaction with others. Thus in relationships the highly neurotic individual can appear confusing or fickle, particularly I believe to a young child as their changing internal moods and difficulties affect behaviour and their responses. Like her apparent vulnerability this required the child me to be especially sensitive and responsive to Mother's needs, in order to ensure Mother felt safe and so in turn able to provide security for me. To realize this, I had to behave in a manner that made her comfortable and secure… after all Mother's wellbeing lay with me, a great responsibility for a young child. So I became her special good little boy to meet her expectations and be someone who wouldn't let her down, of course such a commitment and undertaking results in little chance for individual development and autonomy. Inevitably then there was to some extent a denial of my true nature, which carried over into my developing personality; plus of course if one feels obliged to act continuously in particular way… resentment is very apt to develop. To her credit my mother did realised to some extent that she had made me, as she viewed it too dependent upon her. She thus tried rather unsuccessfully in the years that followed to get me to join organizations such as the cubs and in general to acquire friends. Unfortunately, the die was cast and my earliest years continued to determine the older child, and so I stubbornly remained mother fixed and fearful of the outside world.

In order to demonstrate the validity of my beliefs concerning my mother's early influence upon me, the following paragraph shows some of the striking similarities between her mode of thinking and mine. Not surprisingly much of what is similar now resides within my raw child complex, and when I (the adult me) experience this material; it has all the characteristic oddness and obsessional value that makes intrusive ideas so difficult to ignore and just dismiss.

A) So Mother is fearful, indecisive and panicky, she is afraid of being alone, the dark, confined places etc. In general, under stress she can decompensate into a vulnerable and super dependent individual.

a) My raw child complex is fearful and panicky and markedly afraid of being alone, although in him this fear is about being away from or without Mother. In general, this part of me is scared of his environment… the fear has a strange comprehensive, yet unknowing feature to it. The consequence of this is that he is constantly anxiously vigilant of his surroundings, and any unwitnessed or unexplained changes cause him to panic.

B) Mother is passive, fearful of rejection and therefore a pleaser. She fears and is critical of self-assertion and certainly of any show of anger, she has strong moral views and tends to feel very guilty about any transgressions.

b) My raw child is fearful of others and thus is a pleaser, and under the influence of this part of me my adult personality is passive and timid. Moreover, I tend to feel guilty and my raw child is extremely guilt prone, this tendency finding expression throughout my childhood in spontaneous fears of punishment, and the carrying out of self-punishments to ward these off (see chapter one).

C) Mother's general fears about anger also found a family outlet, namely her preoccupation with the 'Collins mad eyes' (see chapter one), which supposedly afflicted both my grandfather and father when they were angry.

c) My raw child complex is afraid of being bad especially in mother's view, and he is particularly terrified of his own anger. The internalised fear of developing the same 'mad eyes' has resulted in my raw child being afraid of any bad person or 'power' in case they contaminate him, i.e. he becomes bad too. Moreover, this childish fear has resulted in obsessional ideas of the same nature being thrust upon my adult thinking in certain circumstances, and in general the fear of my anger has compounded my tendency to be a timid and passive adult.

D) A specific example of Mother's concern to do the right thing, and suffer guilt if she doesn't is embodied in her belief of never hurting a fly, an ant or anything if you can prevent it. Thus, for example if she sees a worm or snail crossing the pavement she at once feels obliged to move it out of harm's way and if she doesn't she feels guilty and attempts later (if at all possible) to check if they are indeed ok.

d) In relation to the above my raw child is troubled by exactly the same emotionally charged ideas, the infringement of which leads to guilt and a fear of punishment. In keeping with the other propensities within this complex these ideas too, can appear as intrusions into adult thinking, for example when washing the car, I often feel compelled to remove any insects present first, in case they should be drowned.

From the above it is apparent just now much my developing personality identified with and then internalised my mother's psychopathology. Also apparent from the thread of information throughout this book is just how powerful is my raw child's concern for Mother's welfare. Again and again from my earliest notes onwards, the theme of this concern is shown via fears of my mother dying. These fears personalised in me by association with the following linked ideas.

a) Of leaving mummy in general, because she'd be alone and upset.

b) Can't grow up because mummy would be old then and might die.

c) Generalised fears of loss, loneliness, final separation, death, being alone and of being bad.

With these powerful emotions and fears dominating my raw child personality, the morbid nature of the relationship I had with my mother, is I hope clear. For it is that relationship above all else I believe predisposed me to develop OCD in later life. Thus it is to that period I now turn in this final psychogenic explanation of the aetiology of this disorder in me. But before proceeding I will concede to those who believe there is a genetic component to OCD the possibly I also inherited a proneness to anxiety from my mother. Even if this is so my early environment certainly evoked and exacerbated that tendency. The truth remains that those whose nature you inherit are usually responsible also for one's upbringing, thus one's nature may be further compounded by nurture. As for my other symptoms, (i.e. beyond the anxiety) my particular compulsions and my specific intrusions, these are personal to me due to my early environment and every interaction I've ever had with them since, I hope this book has at least demonstrated that. Other sufferers of course can have symptoms with the similar themes but nevertheless my symptoms remain unique in detail to me, determined as they are by my psychological history.

Thus I maintain that within the first four years of my life the seeds of my later disorder were sown, more specifically this occurring within the super close and exclusive relationship between Mother and me. Here in the complex interaction of her personality with my developing one, the psychopathology that was to haunt me for the rest of my life was laid down. My mother's nature and state of mind during this period, which I have already touched upon, made her super overprotective of me. In addition, her neurotic idiosyncrasies made herself appear vulnerable and needy, which indeed I believe she was. Picking up on and internalising her anxiety made me anxious too, in such a position any child needs reassurance and protection, but my mother's own vulnerability undermined any convincing support. Thus in order to gain the protection I needed, I first had to support

Mother, this I did by becoming her special good little boy within our 'special' relationship, and I believe Mother was not passive in this process, but actively desired it, because it was to her behaviour that reinforced her belief that she was a good and lovable mother... i.e. I was clingy and needy. Supporting Mother, meeting her needs consisted of being super sensitive to her neurotic character, and being the little boy that kept her comfortable. For example, I couldn't have the 'mad eyes' of either Father or Grandfather... Mother didn't like those, and to upset Mother threatened the special relationship. So I was and remained Mother's good and conforming little boy who kept her happy and thus dependable, of course none of this was rationally considered, it just by necessity grew out of my emotional needs of the time. It represents in theoretical terms a certain amount of role reversal; the child needs to take care of Mother first, to ensure she can in turn take care of him.

This then was the essence of the dyadic relationship that dominated my early years; within it although it was by nature restrictive and unhealthy I got by, I was ok the problems to which it predisposed me were yet to become manifest. Nonetheless there was one event during this early period that was to shake my emotional belief in my mother, and leave an enduring traumatic flaw within my psyche. This was the short admission to hospital when I was two for a circumcision. This event with its two nights away from Mother in a strange and distressing environment was viewed by my child personality, as abandonment and betrayal. Even though I had been Mother's special little boy I had been rejected, therefore I must have been bad, and the powerful emotions evoked by this experience were a mix of fear and rage... I both needed my mother and hated her for abandoning me. On returning home the hate and anger were never expressed, I became again Mother's special little boy no doubt trying additionally hard to please her to avoid being rejected and punished again. Of course constantly being a pleaser eventually leads to resentment and further anger, anger that added to that evoked by the hospital trauma. Mother fixed, fearful of the world and feeling responsible for Mother's continued well-being, my child personality never grew up, he couldn't... otherwise Mother would grow old and die, and this resulted in a pseudomaturity as I grew older. Although I was not to experience directly the disturbing and powerful emotions of my raw child personality, during my later childhood, this aspect was to nevertheless greatly shape and influence my development, thus I became a shy, timid and over cautious older child always fearful of being away from home or my parents. The vulnerability of my perceived relationship with my mother was revealed clearly when my brother was born, this event once again aroused the rejection fears of my raw child personality, and in consequence of this at a consciously level (in the 10-year-old me), was a compulsive need in regard to my mother, to continuously say sorry, confess anything I had done wrong and feel in general that I had to do everything she asked of me. Although the older child me felt these compulsive impulses were silly and I was embarrassed when carrying them out, I was neither alarmed by them nor frightened of them. For these early intrusions from my raw child complex were by their nature in keeping with my acknowledged belief system, in short their ideology did not threaten 'the me' I knew. Thus in common with all of my obsessions and compulsions that dominated my childhood (up the age of 15), these were ego-syntonic in nature that is they were in harmony with, or at least tolerable to my conscious personality. Other examples were the intrusive fears of illness and the dread of hospital as a punishment (see chapter one), and the various compulsions linked to these such as the self-punishments I engaged in. It is my belief that these ego-syntonic type intrusions were nothing more than internal communication from my infantile raw child complex to the older child me, reflecting the fears and the general disposition of that child complex.

The next event that was to trigger the rejection fears of my raw child was also the one to leave the lasting legacy of my ego-dystonic symptoms, which were for me emotionally at least, the start of my OCD proper, because their nature forced me to acknowledge that there was something very strange and frightening indeed occurring within me. The event was of course my leaving school at the age of 15; under the influence of shallow adolescent changes I rejected the restrictions of school life and woefully unprepared for the consequences such a decision would have, I left. Within weeks of this catastrophic blunder I began to feel increasingly anxious, which led on to a specific feeling of 'not feeling safe'. Although unknown to me at the time these feelings were the first stirrings of my raw child complex, just as he had been evoked by the birth of my brother, so the act of leaving school did so again, after all it represented growing up and moving on…away from Mother. Undermined by my now active raw child complex my older self also crippled by anxiety could not carry on. Leaving work and refusing to return I broke down in floods of emotion… my child aspect had achieved what he wanted and had returned me to the supposed safety of home. Unfortunately, my mother could no longer see the small child who so wanted the protection of her and the home environment, and I lacking the insight to either explain or even understand the situation for myself, could not enlighten her. So instead of protection and love there was anguish and conflict between us as my mother tried everything to push me back out into world. As a result, the relationship deteriorated, further increasing my anxiety feelings, it was at this point a rage appeared within me that initially at least was solely directed at my mother. I now maintain that this rage so out of character, was an old anger associated with my raw child complex, a rage that had its origin in my early hospital visit. The feelings of rejection and betrayal of the present situation had awakened those

239

belonging to the earlier event, and the anger denied expression then had now returned. Eventually the realization of the hopelessness of the situation at home pushed me back out to work, despite still not understanding why I had run back there in the first place. Feeling abandoned and not daring to mention my distress anymore, my 'not feeling safe' feelings continued unabated while my anxiety levels persistently rose and panic attacks became frequent terrifying episodes. These admittedly common psychiatric symptoms were in me driven by the powerful emotions emanating from my raw child complex, who was by then in a tumult of equally powerful and yet opposite feelings. It was as if I had a child within me who was in the midst of an unrelenting tantrum. Then from the midst of this inner turmoil a new type of intrusive thought began... when as if out of nowhere I began to experience intrusions that were oppositional, challenging and questioning of my existing beliefs and thought patterns. It was as if the very integrity of my personality was now under threat, the aspect of me later named Rebel had appeared.

But what was this ego dystonic part of me, and why had he emerged now or more correctly as stated before re-emerged, for I now recognise Rebel as yet another childlike tendency that has persisted from my past. When compared with my raw child, Rebel appears to have a much simpler disposition as his repertoire of intrusions are limited to one theme, that of being completely opposite in view, inclination or reaction to anything held important or feared by my adult or raw child personalities. Although to be fair he is also capable of just being more, that is to say becoming very angry for example, in situations when I feel just a little annoyed. Any attempt to reason or remonstrate with this complex always ends in complete failure... thus in character he behaves very like a child around about the age of 2, one that is well into that discovery that they possess a will of their own. Children of that age are typically wilful, either doing the opposite to what they're asked or ignoring completely the request. The characteristic negativism of this period, always finding delight in being contrary and perverse is exactly how I experience my Rebel complex, although it still took many years to comprehend and fully trust this insight. Rebel then, just like my raw child complex is a still active fragment of my earlier infantile thinking, if he resembles a child of approximately 2 that is because, this was my age when first these tendencies appeared. This assertion may be verified by my raw child's terror of Rebel, for he of course experienced this rebellious aspect... when he and rebel were my actual current thought patterns. How difficult it would have been for this timid, mother fixed and conforming little child to deal with these natural yet powerfully nonconformist urges. Rebel threatened my raw child's relationship with Mother for he would no longer be Mother's special little boy if Rebel's self-assertion and wilfulness found expression. It is indeed ironic that these were probably the very attributes I required to grow up and start to separate successfully from Mother's influence. Rebel appeared shortly after the traumatic period back at home when I had refused to return to work, the trigger event of leaving school that first evoked my raw child complex was eventually to evoke Rebel also. When my raw child complex perceived my mother's attitude towards the 15-year-old me as lasting rejection and abandonment, the constant need to be Mother's special little boy finally collapsed and the old rage linked to my mother reappeared, and along with it the Rebel child tendency (long denied expression) re-emerged also. Intrusions into my adult awareness now reflected Rebel's age and nature as well as those of my raw child. Perhaps if Rebel had been effectively incorporated within my developing personality at the age of his original appearance, the 15-year-old me would not have run away from work desperately seeking to remain a child. But this was never to happen, the peculiarities of my early environment and my interaction with it insured the potential self-assertion and robustness latent within Rebel was never allowed the effective expression necessary to make a difference; I remained an emotionally immature child and then adult, under the subtle yet continuous influence of my raw child complex.

In January 2015 I undertook a genetic test (via a mouth swab) because I was interested to find out if I possessed a genetic tendency to be anxious. After all, anxiety is the key emotional component of OCD, and I was quite willing to believe that this underlying propensity may be an inherited trait... perhaps inherited from my anxious mother. Even if this were so I was still convinced that my early environment would have still further compounded the problem, and determined the personal ways it found expression. But in fact when the test returned it indicated no definite marker for anxiety, on the scale provided between 'worrier versus warrior' I showed a mixed (average) response. True I was more towards the worrier end but nevertheless there was no pointer to an inborn inclination to anxiety. This information of course strengthened my view that the underlying causes of my OCD symptoms, unlike most current psychiatric opinion, lay substantially in my early environment. Once my infantile complexes had been reawakened by the trigger event of leaving school and the later rejection by Mother, they persisted and were now active within my psyche at a level, which allowed them to intrude into my 'normal' everyday thinking. The stage was now set for the development of the symptoms that were to blight my life from this period onwards. When these first appeared they were I believe in their purest form, and by that I mean the content of a particular intrusive thought and accompanying emotional feel, significantly represented the particular nature of the infantile complex that evoked it. But this state of affairs tends not to remain, for intrusive thoughts tend to continue to evolve both in the complexity of the unbidden ideas themselves, and in the extent of the situations that trigger them. This occurs because once the intrusive material is perceived at a conscious level there is a response to it and an interaction with it. Possible responses are fear, guilt feelings, and checking compulsions etc. and these later develop into prohibitions and limitations being placed on oneself and similar situations. These all too natural reactions, I believe, cause the original symptoms to advance into other areas of one's life by association, while the complexity of the responses build in turn further complexity into the symptoms. This takes place because the interaction of course operates both ways, and hence in communicating with my adult thought processes, my infantile aspects are themselves subjected to adult material that would have not been present when they developed. With this material together with my conscious efforts to fend off the intrusions the infantile complexes themselves react, and subsequent intrusions may reflect this. For example, my fears of my violent impulses led to consciously considered concerns about anything that could conceivably be used as a weapon, so as stated before I developed a phobia of hammers and other tools. Despite my fears or more likely because of them, very quickly images of using such 'weapons' appeared in my sudden intrusive impulses. My Rebel complex in keeping with his infantile propensity to do just the opposite had contrived a symptom change… urging now the very action I feared. Of course my raw child personality is just as capable of such interactions, although as the reader will well know by now, these are very different in nature as they reflect a fearful and timid disposition. A good example would be my adult and obviously justifiable concerns about mental illness; these concerns always evoke a far deeper and older emotional response, of illness associated with fears of hospital, rejection and abandonment as my raw child reacts to this new threat, in old ways determined by his past traumas and infantile beliefs.

At this point the reader may justifiably ask, has all this insight and understanding into the underlying structure of my OCD resulted in a therapeutic gain? Have I been able to reduce or prevent certain symptoms, or indeed have I cured myself? Well as this book records a lifetime of suffering I offer of course no method of curing OCD. The disorder has in me continued to follow a rather typical course, waxing and waning throughout my life in response to the external stressors that any life brings, and although there were periods when I was virtually unaware of it... symptoms would always return. Anyway the idea of a complete cure is for me impossible, for my OCD isn't just an isolated defect that can be plucked out of the mind and discarded... it's a part of me and perhaps although infantile in nature, an important part if its development had not been arrested. Despite that belief and thus limitation, my self-knowledge has nonetheless still provided me with a certain ability to lessen the emotional impact and intensity of my symptoms, in other words I believe personal insight has enabled me to live better with this disorder than would have been otherwise possible. One definite gain insight provides is with one's relationship to the symptoms, especially the intrusive thoughts... experiencing these sudden unbidden and unrecognised intrusions particularly when they are of a nature wholly contrary and repugnant to one's known character, almost 'instinctively' evokes intense anxiety. After all, this disturbing aberration appears within you and seems to threaten the very integrity of one's sense of self. In response, one's rational adult mind is filled with self-questioning and doubts, where do these ideas come from, am I going mad, am I dangerous now, will these thoughts force me to act on them etc. Lacking understanding fuels these fears and it was only after I began to comprehend the true nature and origin of these intrusions, as infantile tendencies in me explainable in terms of one's personal life history, did I start to view my symptoms as less strange and frightening. In regard to Rebel specifically I have noticed that if I act in a more robust and assertive way in certain situations rather than in a way more akin to my timid raw child. Then the spontaneous intrusions of violence tend not to occur; it is as if the Rebel aspect of me acts in my stead if I (the adult) fail to adequately stand up for myself. As for my raw child, knowing his vulnerabilities and sensitivities has enabled me to more effectively support and protect this vulnerable aspect of myself, either by avoiding certain trigger situations (not usually practical nor easy to do) or by being the able,

confident and encouraging adult to this aspect of myself...
that he so needed in my (or his) formative years.

Unfortunately, there is, I have to admit, one serious
drawback to this therapeutic approach; it can take a long
time (in my case, at least 20 years) to gain the necessary
level of insight to enable the correct inner support to be
given. Nonetheless, I still believe that although there are
other methods for treating the OCD symptomatology, if
one wants to truly understand the disorder in personal
terms, there is only one method available, and that is to
confront and strive to comprehend its many facets using a
psychodynamic framework. Again, the caveat applies that
this is likely to be a long drawn out process, which
requires much dedication and sheer hard work... for the
underlying structure in such a complex disorder as OCD
will not in my experience reveal itself easily. Also in the
very process of confronting one's symptoms and
disassembling them, there is a real possibility of the
disorder escalating in general; the reader may remember
(chapter 5) that one of the trigger events that provoked a
period of heightened symptoms, was merely reading
through my old notes, and this occurred again and again
while writing this book. Certainly anyone considering an
insight-based therapy should be ready for at least
increased anxiety during the initial stages. To all those
who wish to follow that path I wish them good luck, the
hard work and perhaps additional suffering should I
believe be well repaid by the gains to be achieved in self-

awareness and understanding. Remember these attributes will continue to serve whenever symptoms reappear and whatever their nature… be they old 'friends' or indeed new constructions. For once you know and understand fully the origins of the disorder; the superstructure of developing ideas and emotions built upon this remains amenable to the same understood principles. To the many others who have no intention of undertaking such therapy be they fellow sufferers or not, I hope my person journey has for some provided just some inkling of what may possibly lay beneath OCD symptomatology. While for all readers I hope it has at least been as interesting and perhaps in parts as enlightening a read… as it was for me to research and write it. I will leave you with this last thought, once you have come to accept one's symptoms are but the proverbial tip of the iceberg, a quest to discover more of the vast bulk beneath is I believe the only therapeutic option for some.

BIBIOGRAPHY

I have found aspects of the following books invaluable in my quest to understand OCD; unfortunately, many I fear will be out of print now.

Dibs (in search of self)
By Virginia M. Axline First Published 1964
ISBN 0-14-013459-X

The integrity of the personality
By Anthony Storr First Published 1960

Human Aggression
By Anthony Storr First Published 1968

Jung (selected writings)
Selected & introduced by Anthony Storr First Published 1983
ISBN 0-00-636415-2

Anxiety and Neurosis
By Charles Rycroft First Published 1968

Childhood and Adolescence
By J.A. Hadfield First Published 1962

Dreams and nightmares
By J.A. Hadfield First Published 1954

A population of selves (a therapeutic exploration of personal diversity)
By Erving Polster First Published 1995
ISBN 0-7879-0076-1

The psychology of Interpersonal behaviour
By Michael Argyle First Published 1967

Medicine, mind & magic
By Guy Lyon. Playfair First Published 1985
ISBN 0-85030-588-8

Jungian psychiatry
By Heinrich Karl Fierz First Published 1991
ISBN 3-85630-521-1

The Survival Papers (applied Jungian psychology)
By Daryl Sharp First Published 1990
ISBN 0-572-01585-2

The Jungian Experience (analysis and individuation)
By James A. Hall First Published 1986
ISBN 0-919123-25-2

Memories, Dreams, Reflections
By C.G. Jung First Published (in U.K) 1963
ISBN 0-00-654027-9

Two Essays on Analytical Psychology
By C.G. Jung First Published 1956
ISBN 0-691-01782-4

Psychiatric Studies
By C.G. Jung First Published 1957
ISBN 0-691-01855-3 pbk

Man and his Symbols
Conceived and edited by Carl Jung First Published 1964
ISBN 0 330 25321 2

A Life of One's Own
By Marion Milner First Published 1934
ISBN 978-0-415-55065-9

Though Paediatrics to Psychoanalysis
By D.W. Winnicott First Published 1958

Images of Trauma (from hysteria to P.T.S.D)
By David Healy First Published 1993
ISBN 0-571-16326-12

Introduction to Psychotherapy (an outline of psychodynamic principles and practice) Third Edition
First Published 1979
By Anthony Batman, Dennis Brown and Jonathan Pedder
ISBN 0-415-20569-7

The Normal Child (some problems of the early years and their treatment)
Sixth Edition First Published 1953
By Ronald S. Illingworth

The Stranger in the Mirror (Dissociation the hidden epidemic)
By Maxine Schnall First Published 2001
ISBN 978-0-06-095487-1

Out of the dark
By Linda Caine & Robin Royston First Published 2003
ISBN 0-552-14869-5

The Selected Melanie Klein
Edited by Juliet Mitchell First Published 1986
ISBN 0-14-055209-X

The Gift of Therapy (reflections of being a therapist)
By Irvin D. Yalom First Published 2002
ISBN 0-7499-2373-3

Love's Executioner (and other tales of psychotherapy)
By Irvin D. Yalom First Published 1989
ISBN 0-14-012846-8

Taking Control of OCD (inspirational stories of hope and recovery)
Edited by David Veale and Rob Willson First Published 2011
ISBN 978-1-84901-401-4

Break free from OCD
By Dr Fiona Challacombe, Dr Victoria Bream Oldfield and Professor Paul Salkovskis
ISBN 978-0-09-193969-4 First Published 2011

Sigmund Freud
1: Introductory Lectures on Psychoanalysis This Edition 1973
ISBN 0 14 02.1736.3

Sigmund Freud
2: New Introductory Lectures on Psychoanalysis This Edition 1973
ISBN 0 14 02.1736.3

Sigmund Freud
Joseph Breuer
3: Studies on Hysteria This Edition 1974
ISBN 0 14 02.1737 1

Sigmund Freud
The Interpretation of dreams This Edition 1976
ISBN 0 14 02.1738X

Sigmund Freud
8: Case Histories 1 'Dora' and 'Little Hans' This Edition
1977
ISBN 0 14 02.1742 8

Sigmund Freud
9: Case Histories 2 'Rat Man', Schreber, 'Wolf Man' This
Edition 1979
ISBN 0 14 02.1743 6

Sigmund Freud
10: On Psychopathology This Edition 1979
ISBN 0 14 02.1744 4

Sigmund Freud
A General Selection
Edited by John Rickman First Published 1937

**The Tyranny of Magical Thinking (the child's world
of belief and adult neurosis)**
By George Serban First Published 1982

The Psychology of Moral Behaviour
By Derek Wright First Published 1971

Children's Minds
By Margaret Donaldson First published 1978
ISBN 978-0-00-686122-5

Children under Stress
By Sula Wolff First published 1969

A Secure Base
By John Bowlby First published 1988
ISBN 978-0-415-35527-8

Attachment and Loss
By John Bowlby First Published 1969
ISBN 0-7126-7471-3

The Dark Side of the Inner Child (the next step)
By Stephen Wolinsky First Published 1993
ISBN 1-883647-002

Reclaiming the inner child
Edited by Jeremiah Abrams First Published 1991
ISBN 1-85274-118-X

Discover your sub-personalities (our inner world and the people in it)
By John Rowan First Published 1993
ISBN 0-415-07366-9

A Piagetian Model of Character Structure
By A.J. Malerstein & Mary Ahern First Published 1982
ISBN 0-9644089-0-2

Obsessive-Compulsive Disorder (OCD)
Manifestation, theory and treatment
Psychoanalytic inquiry (volume 21, number 2, 2001)
Editor-in-chief Joseph Lichtenberg First Published 2001

The Presenting Past (4th edition)
By Michael Jacobs First Published 2012
ISBN 978-0-33-524718-9